GCSE

Health and Social Care

Teacher's Resource File

Elizabeth Haworth
Carol Forshaw

Heinemann Educational Publishers,
Halley Court, Jordan Hill, Oxford OX2 8EJ
A division of Harcourt Education

Heinemann is a registered trademark of Harcourt Education Limited

First published 2002
2005 2004 2003 2002
10 9 8 7 6 5 4 3 2

A catalogue record for this book is available from the British Library on request.

ISBN 0 435 47106 6

Pages typeset by 🖝\ Tek-Art, Croydon, Surrey
Printed and bound in Great Britain by Athenaeum Press Ltd, Gateshead

Tel: 01865 888058   www.heinemann.co.uk

Websites
There are links to relevant websites in this book. In order to ensure that the links are up to date, that the links work, and that the sites are not inadvertently linked to sites that could be considered offensive, we have made the links available on the Heinemann website at www.heinemann.co.uk/hotlinks. When you access the site, the express code is 1066T.

Acknowledgements
Every effort has been made to contact copyright holders of material reproduced in this book. Any omissions will be rectified in subsequent printings if notice is given to the publishers.

Contents

Introduction

The aims of the Teacher's Resource File

This Teacher's Resource File has been designed to complement the GCSE Health and Social Care student textbook by providing photocopiable worksheets and student information sheets, as well as lots of advice based on the experience of the authors.

The file aims to complement the student textbook by:

- identifying issues to be considered when setting up the course
- giving suggestions and practical ideas for the delivery of the course
- providing student information sheets which can also be put onto an OHP transparency for a whole class discussion
- providing worksheets which will enforce the facts learned from the textbook, giving opportunities for using Key Skills and suggesting a variety of approaches
- providing a work placement diary
- providing practice exam papers to help students prepare for the externally set Unit 3 test
- identifying useful sources of information.

The accompanying CD-ROM contains teaching notes and worksheets in PDF format, as well as PowerPoint slides of the student information sheets.

Teaching notes and worksheets

For each unit and chapter in the course, this file contains:

Teaching notes: an introduction to the unit, together with teaching tips and suggestions for classroom activities to carry out with your students.

Student information sheets: handouts for students containing information to underpin activities. These sheets may be used as OHTs for class presentations. You will also find PowerPoint slides of some of the information sheets on the CD-ROM.

Worksheets: activities for students to complete and put into their portfolios as evidence of achievement. Many of the worksheets have extension activities designed for students aiming at A grade.

Using the worksheets

The worksheets have been written to test students' knowledge of each chapter and to help them recall ideas already covered in previous chapters. Each worksheet has a cross-reference to the student textbook to help you and your students identify which part of the chapter to use it with; for example, worksheet 1.1 should be used with pages 7–9 of the textbook.

> **Worksheet 1.1**
> pages 7–9

All of the worksheets appear on the CD-ROM in PDF format so that they may be adapted and customised to suit the needs of individual students. There are also extra worksheets available on the CD-ROM.

GCSE Health and Social Care

The qualification is split into three units:

- Unit 1: Health, Social Care and Early Years Provision
- Unit 2: Promoting Health and Well-being
- Unit 3: Understanding Personal Development and Relationships

The course seeks to provide students with sufficient knowledge and skill to enable them to progress into either further education or training or work in health, social care and early years areas.

Assessment

Assessment is by means of a portfolio of evidence and an external test. Units 1 and 2 are assessed by means of a student portfolio which is marked by the teacher/tutor and moderated by the exam board. Guidance for students on how to write a report and a health plan is included in this TRF (see pages 139–43). Unit 3 has an external test which is set and marked by the exam board. Practice exam papers for AQA, Edexcel and OCR for you to give out to your students are supplied on pages 144–72. Marking schemes for all three boards are also provided.

Student portfolios should contain the assignments based on Units 1 and 2. A Work Placement Diary is provided in the Appendices to help the students collect the information they will need to complete assignment 1. Further information on interpreting the awarding bodies' grading criteria can be found in the relevant board's GCSE Health and Social Care specifications.

Student portfolios

The portfolio can have pieces of relevant information inserted in it as the students are taught each unit, but realistically they will only begin to put the assignment together when they have finished the relevant unit of study. The assignments take a lot of time to compile, and it is worth devoting a considerable amount of lesson time to the process; a minimum of six to eight weeks per assignment is suggested.

It is important to emphasise to students the need to signpost each piece of work so that it is clear which of the criteria it is covering; for example, section A could have a large A in the corner of each page. This will help each student see what they have covered, help you mark the work and help the moderator. You could even sub-divide each section of the assessment and label each new section, so that the assignment has even more structure.

Delivering GCSE Health and Social Care

Teaching and learning styles

The GCSE in Health and Social Care lends itself perfectly to using the world of work as an important resource. Taking the students out of school or bringing speakers in will hopefully motivate and interest students because they gain a more tangible sense of what they are learning. It is therefore important that lessons also motivate and enthuse the students.

Students will need to acquire a range of skills to be successful in this subject. For example, they are required to compile a portfolio of assignments which relies on their ability to investigate and report on various topics themselves. In order to encourage the development of these skills, it is a good idea to adopt an approach where students often take the lead in lessons, with the teacher acting as a facilitator.

Portfolio skills

In order to teach the students the skills they will need, it is worth taking the first few weeks to do just that and the Portfolio skills section of this TRF contains worksheets and student information sheets to help you do this. Each worksheet has accompanying teacher's notes which tell you:

- the expected learning outcomes
- what resources you will need
- a suggested lesson structure
- additional suggestions.

Resources

The students will each need a **portfolio**. They will also need a couple of dividers and a pack of plastic document wallets each. If you are short of funds, students can purchase the latter two items themselves. The portfolios need to be kept locked up somewhere, preferably in the room the students mainly work in so that they are accessible when they need them. This might mean purchasing a lockable cupboard.

Leaflets picked up from places such as medical centres, hospitals, social services, the library etc. provide a good source of information, as well as useful addresses to which students can write to ask for additional copies.

Newspapers and magazines are a good source of articles for reference as well as for pictures for students to cut out to use to illustrate their portfolio work.

There are regularly **television programmes** screened in the evening, which look at issues such as the state of the NHS. There are also school programmes on issues such as smoking, drugs, and alcohol. These are worth videotaping as buying pre-recorded tapes can be expensive.

A **digital camera** is useful for recording visits out, speakers in, work placements etc. and can provide valuable evidence for the two portfolio assignments, as well as photos for wall displays.

A **dictaphone** is useful for students to take out and record interviews with care workers or clients or to record information given by speakers – they must ask permission to record first of course.

It is important that students have access to **computers** to conduct research and to word process work, particularly their assignments, as this enhances the presentation of their portfolios. It is also important because vocational courses should be delivered through the use of Key Skills, of which ICT is one.

Students need to be trained in the use of the **Internet**. There is a tendency to type in two words as a search term and then print out page after page of articles that are either irrelevant or difficult to understand. Encouraging students to use a search engine facility such as Google (www.google.co.uk) helps them to define their search more clearly. It is also important to encourage students to restrict their search to UK websites otherwise they will end up with lots of obscure websites produced by establishments all over the world.

Teaching tip

Set up a large crate with a lid in the corner of the room for leaflets, magazines and flyers ready for cutting up by students.

Work placements

It is very important that the vocational nature of the course be reflected in the kinds of activities that students get involved in i.e. they should be encouraged to get out into the world of work. This provides many benefits such as:

- the opportunity to collect information needed for their portfolio assignments
- the opportunity to see what it is really like to work in the area of health, social care and early years, thereby giving the students the chance to decide whether it really is for them
- the opportunity for students to see the structures, workers, qualities, skills and other ideas they have learned about in school as they are in real life, thereby making them more relevant and memorable
- giving the students confidence to use the communication skills they have learned in school.

Planning work placements

Work placements should be planned very carefully. Ideally, the work placements should be as close to school as possible so that students are not having to waste a lot of time travelling or spending a lot of money on bus fares. You might like to check whether there is anyone in your group who suffers financial hardship and make sure that their work placement is as near to school as possible on the grounds that they won't be incurring any extra cost.

You will need to find a number of each kind of workplace, particularly nurseries, as they will only take two or three students at a time. This is because the children might feel intimidated if there were too many helpers in the nursery at once. Even though local nurseries can be found in Yellow Pages, it is worth contacting your careers co-ordinator or LEA Education Business Partnership because they will have a database containing all the places used for work experience which:

- will have been vetted for health and safety
- will be used to having students visit
- will have a contact name and number
- will have the correct insurance cover. If you ring local places yourself they might not be insured.

Once you have your contacts and dates it is a case of ringing them up and explaining what you want. It is then worth making a personal visit to each place just to clarify details and to make sure that you know exactly where each place is to advise the students. It is important that at that visit you give them a copy of the **work placement diary** so that the supervisor knows exactly what the students will be trying to find out (see Appendix 1). This visit should be followed up by a letter setting out the dates, times, numbers of students etc. so that they have it in writing.

Preparing students for work placements

The following checklist will help you to prepare students for work placements.

✓ Students need a printed timetable, giving the dates, times, placement addresses, contact names, telephone numbers and anything else that you think of, well in advance so that they can work out how to get there

✓ Students need to be given the work placement diary (one per placement) and told that they must take it each week

✓ Students should be told that they must ring both the work place and school if they are ill and cannot attend

✓ Students need to be told how important it is that they attend and are punctual

✓ Remind them that they should not be talking about the clients either in or out of school, except within the confines of the Health and Safety Care lessons

✓ Remind them not to make careless remarks, such as referring to someone as an 'old codger' in front of another elderly person

✓ Give each student a pass to carry with them giving the dates and times of the visits so that if they are challenged by authorities such as the police they can prove that they really should be out of school

✓ Tell the students that you will be driving round visiting different places each week and to expect you when they see you. It is important that you do drive round and visit so that not only are the students reassured but the supervisors see that you are interested

✓ Write to the parents to tell them what is happening and that they won't be under your direct supervision. Include a reply slip which asks parents to sign to say that they are happy with the arrangements

✓ Explain to the students that the work placement diary requires them to ask the supervisor's permission before taking photographs in the placement

✓ Talk to the students about what they can expect, especially in residential homes for elderly people who are mentally ill, which can be upsetting

✓ Prepare the staff at the school. Tell them what is happening and explain that the work placements have been arranged so other trips should not be subsequently arranged that clash with the placements dates and times.

After the placements it is important that the students are encouraged to put their diaries and any photos, leaflets, pictures drawn by children etc. straight into their portfolio so that they are safe for when they need them for Unit 1.

Speakers

Inviting speakers into school can help to motivate and interest the students, particularly for Unit 1 when the students need to learn about a variety of jobs. Sending a school letter out to parents can generate a list of people who work in the health, social care and early years settings. A useful source of contacts could be the school nurse or the local Primary Care Trust. It is important to emphasise to speakers that they need to talk at the level of the students and avoid using lots of jargon.

Delivery through Key Skills

Although it is not necessary to test Key Skills, they form a good vehicle for delivering the course. The Key Skills are:

- Communication
- Application of Number
- Information Technology
- Working with Others
- Improving Own Learning and Performance
- Problem Solving.

A grid showing which worksheets use which Key Skills is provided in Appendix 2.

Portfolio skills

Teaching notes

These worksheets have been designed to teach students the skills they need to collect information and evidence for inclusion in their portfolio.

Worksheet 1
Putting together a portfolio of evidence

This worksheet should be distributed to students when you are discussing what will be expected from them at the end of Units 1 and 2.

Worksheet 2
Code of conduct

Learning outcomes
This worksheet aims to teach students:

- To work together as a group
- To be sensitive to the feelings of others

Pre-lesson preparation
- Book a computer suite

Suggested lesson structure
- Ask each student to introduce themselves to the rest of the group, giving their name, some family details and the reason why they chose to study GCSE Health and Social Care – you could do the same to show that you are part of the group
- Explain the nature of the issues which will be covered in the course and the fact that there could be students sitting in the group who might be being affected by some of the issues
- Ask students to write down their own ideas on the worksheet individually

- Instigate class discussion to agree 10 'rules' to form a code of conduct
- Word process the code of conduct

Key issues for inclusion in the discussion
- Confidentiality
- Respect for the views of others
- Respect for the property of others
- All try to contribute
- All allowed to contribute
- Be nice to each other
- Don't pass insensitive comments about, for example, someone's weight or family

Worksheet 3
Collecting evidence

Learning outcomes
This worksheet aims to teach students:

- What we mean by evidence
- Why we need evidence
- Where they can collect evidence from

Suggested lesson structure
- Students answer questions 1–5 in small groups
- Draw out the answers to question 6 in a class discussion
- Students draw the spider diagram individually

Suggested answers
1. Security cameras, mirrors, alarm
2. Video and photographic evidence, eye witness from observation on security mirror
3. Video and photographic evidence
4. (i) Fax, e-mail

   (ii) Photo on poster, television
5. Interview, audiotape answers
6. Word process report, keep tapes of interviews

Worksheet 4
Every picture tells a tale

Learning outcomes

This worksheet aims to teach students:

- the importance of photographic evidence

- how to pick out evidence shown in a photograph

- how to use a digital camera if one is available

Pre-lesson preparation

- Ask students to bring in interesting photos e.g. from magazines, postcards, family photos etc.

Resources

- A selection of photographs/pictures mounted on card to pass round for students to comment on, for example, war veterans on D-Day, Princess Diana in front of the Taj Mahal.

- Digital camera

- Sugar paper, scissors, glue

- Selection of pictures from magazines/ postcards as spares for those who forget to bring any in

- Computer suite

Suggested lesson structure

Group work

- Show the students the mounted pictures

- Ask them what they show

- Tell them what else they show if you know the background, for example, the beautiful woman in front of a famous beauty spot is in fact Princess Diana, posing alone in front of a monument built for love as her marriage to Prince Charles is crumbling

- Show students how to use digital camera if one is available

In pairs, if a digital camera is available:

- Students take it in turns to go round the school and take two photos of aspects of the school they are proud of and two of aspects they are ashamed of

- Print out the photos, mount them on sugar paper and label them with catchy captions

- Do the worksheet

Worksheet 5
Conducting a survey

Learning outcomes

This worksheet aims to teach students:

- How to conduct a survey

- The usefulness of a survey as a method of collecting opinions or facts from a group of people in order to predict the opinions or facts of a larger group of people

- The limitations of a survey – success depends on the number and cross-section of people questioned

- The difference between a survey and a questionnaire – a questionnaire focuses more on collecting statistics whereas a survey is used to form a more general view

Resources

- Computer suite

Suggested lesson structure

In a group
- Conduct survey

- Collate results

Individually
- Write report

Class discussion
- Compare results

- Answer questions on worksheet

Worksheet 6
Get it taped

Learning outcomes

This worksheet aims to teach students:

- The advantages and disadvantages of using audiotapes

- The advantages and disadvantages of using videotapes

- How to use recording equipment

Pre-lesson planning

- Set students the task of interviewing an elderly person as per the worksheet within a week

Resources
- Video camera
- Video tapes
- Cassette recorder with microphone and tape to book out to students who don't have access to one

Suggested lesson structure
Group work
- Students allocated roles and time to prepare for interviews
- Allocate a different topic to each group (see below)
- Students conduct the video interviews as per the instructions on the worksheet

Individually
- Answer the questions on the worksheet

Class discussion
- Brainstorm advantages and disadvantages

Key issues for the discussion
- Leisure time at the weekend
- Family holiday
- Family life
- School uniform
- Hobbies
- Smoking in public places
- Legalising cannabis
- Drinking and driving – zero tolerance

Suggested answers
- Audiotapes – self-conscious, transcribe at leisure, accurate, don't worry about what I look like
- Videotapes – self-conscious, worry about appearance, position of limbs etc., accurate, transcribe at leisure, more evidence from body language

Worksheet 7
In your own words

Learning outcomes
This worksheet aims to teach students:
- That plagiarism means taking and using others people's thoughts, writings or inventions as their own

- How to rewrite an piece of information in their own words

Resources
- A selection of articles cut out of magazines, preferably all different, on a cross-section of topics
- Some harder articles, maybe printed off the Internet, for extension activity

Suggested lesson structure
- Teacher explanation of method as per worksheet
- Individual work using article and worksheet

Worksheet 8
Talk it over

Learning outcomes
This worksheet aims to teach students:

- The key points to delivering a talk well i.e. preparation, visual aids, bullet pointed notes, correct volume and projection, correct pace, timing, use of notes, eye contact, varied tone, answering questions
- To listen carefully to, and evaluate, the talks of others
- The need to reflect honestly on their own performance
- To listen to constructive criticism of their own performance in order to improve

Pre-lesson planning
Ask students to prepare a 5-minute talk on any subject that interests them which is to include a visual aid of some sort. Topics could be a hobby, a famous person or a film. Give students a date and time for them to deliver their talk to the rest of the group. Tell them they will be marked on the points listed in the learning outcomes and will be expected both to evaluate their own talk and listen to others comment on their talk.

Suggested lesson structure
- Allocate appointments for each talk so that there are maybe two at the beginning of each lesson for a number of lessons, so that students don't get bored and restless

- Ask the student to deliver their talk while you and the rest of the group completes the worksheet 'Talk it over'

- Ask the student to answer any questions asked at the end and say honestly how they thought it went at the end of the questions

- Ask the others students to say what was good and not so good about the talk. Stress the need to be constructive in their criticism

- Discuss whose is best and why

- If time allows, repeat with an audio tape (this is not mentioned on the worksheet in case time does not permit this)

- Discuss which was easier, video or audio

Homework

Take bullet point notes while watching a television programme at home. Write a report on the programme from the notes.

Worksheet 9
Make a note

Learning outcomes

This worksheet aims to teach students how to make accurate notes from television, video or audio recordings

Resources

- Television

- Video recorder

- Short video, about 10 minutes long, on a factual topic such as birds or bones

- Cassette recorder

- Short audiotape on a factual topic

Suggested lesson structure

Individual work

- Students complete the first part of the worksheet

Group work

- Students watch a short video and make notes on the worksheet. Teacher also takes some notes in bullet point form.

- After a couple of minutes stop the tape and ask a few students to read what they've written so far.

- Read out the bullet points you've made so far so they can see whether they are on the right track.

Individual work

- Students write up their notes on the back of the worksheet

Group work

- Select two or three students to read out what they have written.

Worksheet 10
Find it out

Learning outcomes

This worksheet aims to teach students to:

- Be selective when accessing information on the Internet

- Use a search engine

- Draw mind maps

Pre-lesson planning

- Book a computer suite

Resources

- Plain white paper (A4 and/or A3)

Suggested lesson structure

Teacher input

- Explain to students about not printing off every obscure article which has a brief reference to their topic and which is either irrelevant, at a level way above their needs or both

- Explain how to use a search engine

- Explain how to draw a mind map as per worksheet

Individually

- Students research on the Internet

- Students draw a mind map with the information they have found

- Students answer question/s on worksheet

Worksheet 11
A plan of action

Learning outcomes

This worksheet aims to teach students:

- The importance of planning any event carefully and thoroughly

- How to action plan

Pre-lesson planning

- Decide on a realistic activity for the group to plan from the ones on the worksheet or one of your own

- Write a list of tasks needed to plan the activity so that you can plug any gaps in the group discussion. Include tasks such as setting a date, asking the head's permission, designing an out of school pass etc.

Resources

- Copies of the action plan sheet

Suggested lesson structure

Group work

- Using the worksheet, discuss Dolly Dreamer and Day Tripper

- Explain the action plan sheet

- Give the group a task to plan, as suggested in the worksheet

Worksheet 12
A balanced diet

Learning outcomes

This worksheet aims to:

- Give students the chance to put into practice some of the skills they have learned

- Give students a chance to practice a short assignment and learn from their mistakes

Suggested lesson structure

- Give students about two weeks of lessons to complete this assignment.

- Mark it using the balanced diet assessment sheet

- Students can put the assignment, complete with the assessment sheet, in the portfolio ready to be an appendix to the Unit 2 assignment

Units 1 and 2 of the GCSE Health and Social Care (Double Award) are assessed by means of a portfolio of evidence. The following list gives some ideas and tips on how to make your portfolio attractive and easy for the assessor to mark.

- Word process as much as you can – it looks better, is easier to read and can be corrected at a later date.

- Save everything you do on a computer until your teacher tells you that you are no longer allowed to make any alterations to your portfolio.

- Include a title page stating the name of the course – GCSE Health and Social Care - and your name.

- Produce a front cover for Unit 1 that says 'Unit 1: Health, Social Care and Early Years Provision'.

- Produce a front cover for Unit 2 that says 'Unit 2: Promoting Health and Well-being'.

- Remember to collect any free leaflets or magazine articles that you see on the topic of health and well-being – they may come in useful when you write an assignment, as both a source of information and as illustrations.

- Make sure that you insert clear headings for each section, in a readable font.

- Use sub-headings to break up each section.

- Illustrate your assignments so that they are colourful and attractive to look at – you could do this by using Clip Art in Word or by cutting pictures out of leaflets, magazines etc.

- Include as much detail as you can – the more detail you include the better your mark will be. However, do not include detail that is not relevant. Read the details of the task you have to do very carefully and write up each part in the order given in the instructions.

- Make sure you clearly identify your sources of information.

- Write a list of sources of information at the end. For example, if you have used any books, include the name of the author(s), the year it was published, the title of the book, the publisher and the place of publication e.g.

  Forshaw, C. & Haworth, E. (2002) *GCSE Health and Social Care* (Oxford: Heinemann).

- Write any information that you gather in your own words – you will not gain marks for chunks of work copied out of the textbook or printed out from the Internet or a CD-ROM.

- When you have finished each assignment and your teacher has said it is OK, number the pages and add a contents page to go straight after the title page for that unit.

- Finally, read through your work again to make sure it makes sense and check for errors – even if you have used a spelling and grammar checker, mistakes can still slip through.

Code of conduct

You will be spending a lot of time over the next couple of years with other members of your Health and Social Care group. During that time you will be discussing issues that either already affect your life or will do so eventually, whether directly or indirectly, through one of your family or friends or someone you don't know very well. The issues will range from those such as alcohol drugs and smoking to relationships. It is important that every member of the group feels free to speak and express an opinion or share an experience. Think about how you would like the group to work together.

1. Write down a list of 10 'rules' for the group, such as 'No-one is to repeat anything discussed within the group'.

    1. _____
    2. _____
    3. _____
    4. _____
    5. _____
    6. _____
    7. _____
    8. _____
    9. _____
    10. _____

2. Have a group discussion and share your ideas. Agree as a group the most important ten rules and write them down here.

    1. _____
    2. _____
    3. _____
    4. _____
    5. _____
    6. _____
    7. _____
    8. _____
    9. _____
    10. _____

3. Using a computer, word process the rules, making them look as attractive as possible. Put them in the front of your folder or book. Make sure you stick to them.

Remember that it is important to treat others as you would like to be treated yourself.

Collecting evidence

In order to put together assignments for your portfolio you will have to collect information and provide evidence.

Imagine your group has been given the job of setting up a security system at a music shop to stop thieves during both day and night.

1. List the measures you would take, including a sketch of the shop layout.

Now think about the following scenarios.

2. If a shoplifter was caught, how would your system prove them guilty of theft?

_____

_____

_____

3. If a gang broke in at night and stole a lorry load of computer games and consoles, how would your system prove them guilty of theft?

_____

_____

_____

4. If something in your system captured an image of one of the thieves, how could the police communicate that image with (i) other police forces and (ii) the public in an attempt to catch them? List as many ways as you can.

_____   _____

_____   _____

_____   _____

5. Once one or all of the thieves are in police custody, how will the police get the thieves' version of events at the time of the robbery?

_____

_____

_____

6. How will the police record the evidence?

7. It is suspected that the gang has been involved in other thefts going back a number of years. What sources of information might the police look at to help them find evidence to support their suspicions?

8. The police feel they have enough evidence to convict the thieves and the thieves stand trial in court. What sources of evidence might the police present in court?

9. The thieves each get five years in prison. You feel that your security group has done a good job but want to know what the local people feel about the security measures you have set up. If their opinions are favourable you will be able to quote them in your publicity to get more custom. How could you find out what the public think?

10. Think about your answers. As a group answer the following questions:

- **What** do we mean by evidence?

- **Why** do we need evidence?

- **Where** can we collect evidence?

- Are there any **sources** of evidence that you forgot about when you were answering the questions?

Extension activity

   1. Write the words **'Sources of evidence'** in the middle of a plain piece of paper. Now construct a spider diagram to show the sources of evidence that you can use when you need to produce an assignment.

   2. Collect enough evidence to write a report on one of the large local care settings near you e.g. walk-in-centre, residential home, nursery, or hospital.

1. Photographs have many purposes. Write as many as you can think of here:

_____

_____

_____

_____

_____

_____

2. When people look at the same photograph, they might notice different things about that photograph. It is therefore important that no assumptions are made when a photograph is used as evidence, as shown in the diagrams below:

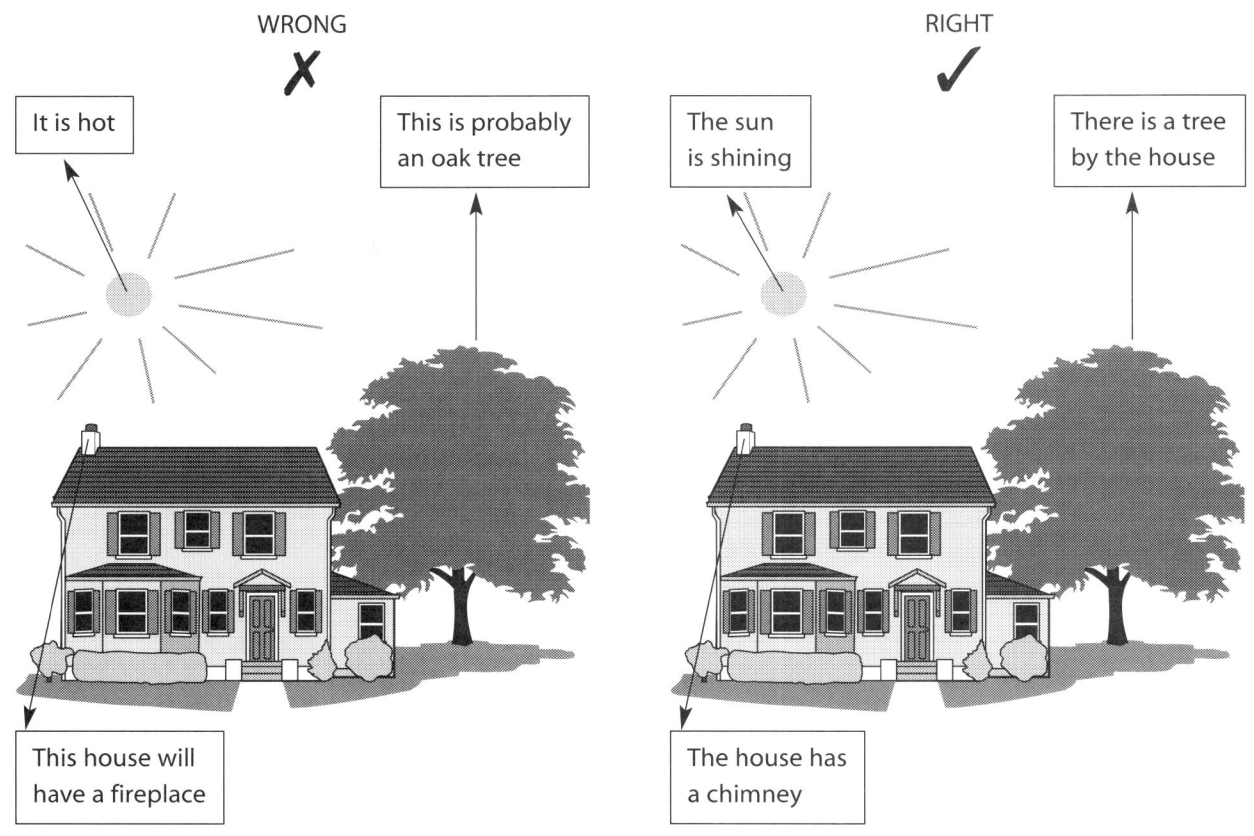

WRONG ✗

It is hot

This is probably an oak tree

This house will have a fireplace

RIGHT ✓

The sun is shining

There is a tree by the house

The house has a chimney

Activity

▷ Stick the photos/pictures/postcards that you have brought in on a piece of plain white paper and label it with facts that several people can see just by looking at the photo.

Repeat this with other pictures and/or photos.

Conducting a survey

1. In a group, answer the following questions:

   (a) What is a survey?

   _____

   _____

   (b) Give an example of when you might use a survey.

   _____

   _____

   (c) What is a questionnaire?

   _____

   _____

   (d) Give an example of when you might use a questionnaire.

   _____

   _____

2. In a small group, conduct a survey on what students in your school eat at lunchtime so that you can find out what proportion of students eat a balanced diet. Decide:

   • How many students to ask   _____

   • Whom to ask (those from one year group? A cross-section of year groups?

   _____

   • The questions to be asked (write these on a different piece of paper)

   • The deadline for completion   _____

3. Collect all the information you need and produce a report which presents your findings clearly and simply. You need to include at least one bar chart or graph.

4. Compare your results with those of other groups. Are they exactly the same? If not, why not?

   _____

   _____

   _____

5. Answer the following questions:

   (a) How is a survey useful as a source of evidence?

   _____

   (b) What are the disadvantages of relying on a survey as a source of evidence?

   _____

   _____

(c) Do you think your survey gave a good enough cross-section of information to be able to predict a general pattern of eating habits of students in your school?

_____

_____

(d) How would you improve your survey if you were to repeat this exercise?

_____

_____

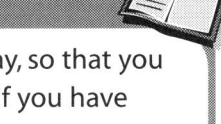

Extension activity

▷ With a partner, design a questionnaire to find out what students eat on a Saturday, so that you can decide what proportion of the students eat a balanced diet. Word process it if you have access to a computer. Compare your questionnaire with another group and decide which would generate the most relevant information in a clear useful way.

Get it taped

It is often hard when you are interviewing someone to ask a question, make notes of the answer given, ask another question and so on. One way to make the process easier is to record the interview, either on audiotape or videotape.

Activity 1: audio recording

Ask an elderly person, aged 65+, if you can interview them about how different the lifestyle of a 16-year-old today is in comparison with when they were 16. You must ask permission to audiotape them. Then listen to the tape and write a summary of the points made, in bullet points, of the interview.

Activity 2: video recording

In a group of three, decide who will be the interviewer, the interviewee and the video camera operator. One member of the group interviews another one of your group about, for example, what they do in their leisure time at the weekend. The interviewer should prepare about 20 questions to ask them. The third member of the group videos the interview.

a) Play the video back and comment on things that went well and things that didn't go so well.

b) Change roles, pick another topic and repeat the process until everyone has had a go at all three roles. Other topics might be a family holiday, family life, school uniform or a hobby.

Now answer the following questions.

1. What were the advantages of using an audio recording rather than a video recording?

_____

_____

_____

2. What were the disadvantages of using an audio recording rather than a video recording?

_____

_____

_____

Extension activity

▷ 1. Think of three situations when both audio recording and video recording would not be useful.

_____

_____

2. What alternative approach could you use?

_____

_____

In your own words

It is very important when you are producing an assignment to write any information you find in your own words. If you simply copy from a book, the Internet or any other service you are plagiarising the information. One way to avoid plagiarism is to:

- read through the article and decide what different key areas are covered
- write a list of headings for those key areas
- read through the information and write bullet points by each heading
- put the article to one side
- rewrite the information in full sentences using your bullet points.

HEADACHES

What causes different types of headaches?
A dull throbbing pain is caused by the arteries in the skull dilating, brought on by hangovers, caffeine or low blood sugars. A sharper pain can be the result of eye strain, stress, injury and sinus problems leading to muscles around the base of the skull contracting. A migraine headache can be brought on by hormone fluctuation and is often accompanied by blurred vision and nausea.

Making it better
It is better to find and treat the cause of headaches rather than just take painkillers. Eating bananas, which are rich in potassium, can help a hangover headache; alcohol dehydrates the body and causes potassium to be lost as well. Potassium is needed to balance the fluids in the body. Caffeine can be cut out of your diet and drinking a lot of water can help reduce the withdrawal symptoms. Eating a breakfast that slowly releases carbohydrates, such as fruit, can treat low blood sugars caused by hunger.

The notes you might make would look like this:

Causes of headaches

Dull throbbing – arteries dilating, base of skull, hangovers, caffeine, low blood sugars

Sharp pain – eye strain, stress, injury, sinuses

Migraine – hormones, blurred vision, nausea

Treatments

Hangover – bananas, potassium loss, alcohol, dehydration, balance fluids

Caffeine – withdrawal symptoms, drink water

Low blood sugars – hunger, breakfast, slow release, carbohydrates, fruit

1. Use the notes above to rewrite the article above.

2. Your teacher will provide you with an article from a magazine. Use this method to rewrite the article in your own words.

Extension activity

▷ Your teacher will give you a more complicated article to rewrite, using the method above.

Talk it over

You are each going to give a 5-minute presentation, using at least one visual aid e.g. a photograph, a certificate, a trophy or medal, to illustrate a point. Listen carefully to each talk and fill in a line of the table below for each talk. Fill in a line for yourself after you have done your own talk.

Mark out of ten	Answered questions well?	Other points e.g. used notes	Length of talk	Made eye contact?	Too fast/ slow/ just right?	Too loud/ quiet/ just right?	Visual aids e.g. photos etc.	Covered subject?	Topic	Name

One source of information is recordings, whether they be video, audio or for television.

1. Look at the descriptions below and decide which best matches you when you watch a video at school and are asked to take notes. Write down the advantages and disadvantages of each method.

    Description 1

    As soon as I hear something that I think is important, I write it down as a complete sentence.

Advantages	Disadvantages

    Description 2

    I don't make any notes at the time, except for the odd word. I write up everything I remember about the video afterwards.

Advantages	Disadvantages

    Description 3

    I note down bullet points and add single words after each bullet point.

Advantages	Disadvantages

2. Now watch the video that your teacher will show you and make notes using bullet points.

3. Using your bullet points, write a summary of the video on the back of this worksheet.

4. From the list above, decide which style of note-taking you will try next time you watch a video.

Find it out

Choose an illness and research it on the Internet using a search engine such as Google. Be very careful – do not print off every article with the name of your selected illness in it.

1. Write down what you want to find out, for example, its technical name, symptoms, causes, treatment, prevention etc. in the table below.

I want to find out	Information

2. Now draw a mind map to illustrate the symptoms and causes of your chosen illness. Do this by writing the name of your illness in the middle of a piece of paper. Put a circle round it (as shown). From the circle, draw an arm outwards and write the word 'symptoms' at the end of it. From the word 'symptoms', draw an arm per symptom and write a symptom at the end of each one. Then draw another arm from the central circle, with the word causes at the end. From there, draw more arms and write a cause at the end of each. Do not write in sentences. Keep going until you have put all the information on your diagram. You have then finished your mind map. It should look a little like a spider with long fingers at the end of each arm!

3. What do you think the advantages are of presenting information in this way?

_____

_____

_____

_____

_____

Find it out (continued)

Extension activity

1. Research another topic, such as the causes of heart disease. This time, draw each arm of the mind map from the centre circle in a different colour and draw pictures instead of writing words. If you wanted to write alcohol you could draw a glass of beer instead.

2. What do you think the advantages are of presenting information like this?

_____

_____

_____

_____

_____

A plan of action

1. Imagine you are going on a sightseeing trip to a capital city in another country. You only have two days to spend there. Are you like:

   (a) Dolly Dreamer, who waits until she gets there and just wanders around, hoping that she will come across something that interests her?

   (b) Day Tripper, who gets hold of a map and guidebook in advance and plans a route for each day that takes him past everything he really wants to see?

   Who do you think will get the most out of the visit - Dolly Dreamer or Day Tripper?

2. One way of planning any visit or event is to action plan. This involves identifying every task that has to be done to complete the plan and filling in the following details on a special action plan sheet:

   • The task – this is the job that needs doing

   • Who – write down the name/s of whoever is going to do the task

   • When by – this is the date by which the task needs to be done

   • Resources – this is a list of anything that is needed to complete the task e.g. access to a telephone line

   • Cost – this is how much it will cost to complete the task. If there is no cost, put n/a for not applicable

   • Success criteria – this is how you can tell that the task has been completed properly

Suggested practice tasks

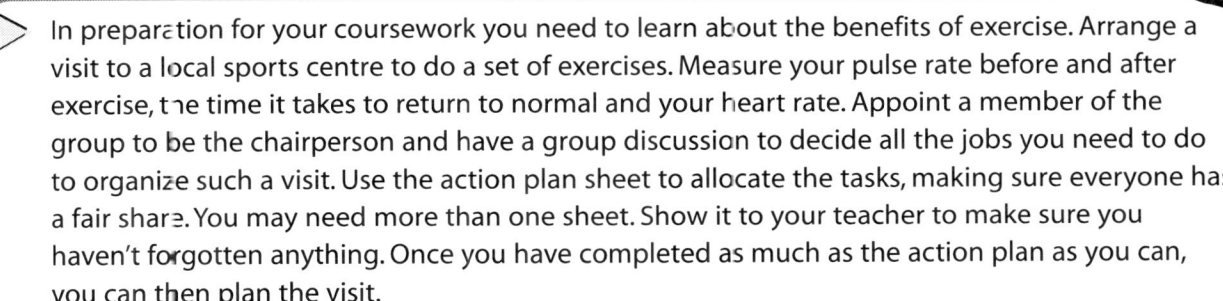

▷ In preparation for your coursework you need to learn about the benefits of exercise. Arrange a visit to a local sports centre to do a set of exercises. Measure your pulse rate before and after exercise, the time it takes to return to normal and your heart rate. Appoint a member of the group to be the chairperson and have a group discussion to decide all the jobs you need to do to organize such a visit. Use the action plan sheet to allocate the tasks, making sure everyone has a fair share. You may need more than one sheet. Show it to your teacher to make sure you haven't forgotten anything. Once you have completed as much as the action plan as you can, you can then plan the visit.

▷ Plan an evening to explain to all the parents and carers of the group the differences between a vocational GCSE course and a more traditional GCSE.

▷ Plan an event to raise money for a charity or a local community group, such as the local nursery.

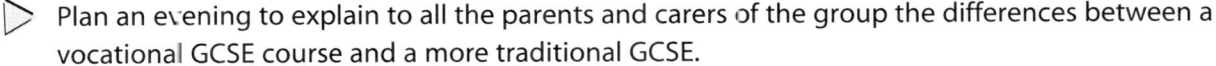

Action plan sheet

Activity to be planned: _____

Task	Who	By when	Resources	Cost	Success criteria

Practice assignment

You are to find out what is meant by a balanced diet. After you have described what this is, you are to plan one day's meals for yourself and show how you have used the information you have found out.

You will need to find out the following information:

1. A list of the main nutrients our body needs.

2. A list of foods that will provide these nutrients.

3. A description of the job that these nutrients do in the body.

When you have found out this information, you should use it for the practical activity, which is to plan a day's meal for yourself (breakfast, lunch and evening meal). You should show how you have used this knowledge to plan a balanced diet for the day.

You should use as many sources of information as you can. These could include:

• textbooks (you can use books from other related subjects e.g. Home Economics, Science)

• magazine articles

• leaflets from the supermarket or food shops

• the Internet.

These sources of information will provide evidence of research activities.

You will gain credit for using a wide variety of sources of information and for using illustrations in your work. Information in your own words will gain more marks than passages copied from a book, even if the copied passage is useful. Illustrations could include your own drawings, pictures from magazines, photographs, etc.

At the end of the work you should include a **bibliography.** This is a list of books (include the title, the author, date published and the publisher), the title of any magazine article and the name of the magazine it came from, the name of a leaflet and who has produced it and the website of any Internet site that you have used.

Balanced diet assignment assessment sheet

Student name: _____

Food groups and their use in the body (one mark for name of food group, one for what it does)

Food group		Possible points	Points awarded
Protein		2	
Carbohydrate	– Sugars	2	
	– Cereals	2	
Fat		2	
Calcium		2	
Iron		2	
Vitamin A		2	
Vitamin B		2	
Vitamin C		2	
Vitamin D		2	
Fibre		2	
Total points		22	

Foods providing the nutrients (one mark per food correctly identified, up to maximum in possible points)

Food group		Possible points	Points awarded
Protein		4	
Carbohydrate	– Sugars	3	
	– Cereals	3	
Fat		5	
Calcium		2	
Iron		2	
Vitamin A		2	
Vitamin B		2	
Vitamin C		2	
Fibre		3	
Vitamin D		2	
Total points		30	

The meal plan for the day

	Possible points	Points awarded
Days meals included	8	
Balanced	8	
Reasons for choice of meals	8	
Total points	24	

Other points

	Possible points	Points awarded
Quality of ICT	6	
Accuracy re. SPAG	6	
Quality of illustrations	6	
Bibliography	6	
Total points	24	

100 marks available

Total points awarded _____ Grade _____

Unit 1   Health, social care and early years provision

Overview

This unit can be quite difficult for the students due to some of the complicated structures within the health, social care and early years services. For this reason, Unit 1 is perhaps best left until after Unit 2, which covers many topics that are relevant to the students as they are growing up. Unit 1 is divided into five chapters.

Chapter 1 – Care needs of major client groups

This chapter looks at who needs to use care services and why. It describes the major client groups – if you have taught GNVQ Foundation please note that babies and children have been put together and the fifth client group is now disabled people. This chapter also looks at social policy goals, how health and local authorities assess the care needs of local populations to decide which services are needed and the reasons why the different client groups use the available services.

Activity

Ask students to find reports on the various Policy Action Teams (PATs) by doing a search on the Internet. The NHS Plan and the technical supplement to the NHS Plan also provide lots of information on social policy goals. The Department of Health website gives a set of presentation slides containing all the key points about the 'Saving Lives: Our Healthier Nation' document. To access the website, visit www.heinemann.co.uk/hotlinks.

Chapter 2 – Types of care services

This chapter looks at the different organisations and private practitioners that deliver health, social care and early years services. It looks at the different ways services are funded and then goes into the structure of the various services. It is worth bearing in mind that the structure of the NHS, for example, changes quite regularly so the information in the chapter might become out of

date, although it is correct at the time of writing. The chapter then goes on to look at how the different service providers work together to meet client needs and points out that informal carers also provide much care.

Teaching tip

Ask a member of the local Primary Care Trust to come and speak to the students about the structure of the NHS. This will ensure that the information is as up to date as possible.

Chapter 3 – Ways of obtaining care services and barriers to access

This chapter covers the different ways in which people are referred to the different services and the ways in which some people are prevented from using them. It covers a more extensive range of barriers than the GNVQ Foundation. It then goes on to look at ways in which services and clients can try to overcome these barriers and how poor integration of services, rationing and the postcode lottery affect availability of services in a particular area.

Discussion point

Your students will have stories to tell about how lack of access to services has affected members of their family. Newspapers, both national and local, feature articles on the topic of barriers to access almost daily. Ask students to bring in any articles they read and encourage them to debate the key issues in a group.

Teaching tip

The national surveys of NHS patients, available from the NHS, is a useful source of data about the feelings of clients about various aspects of the service provided by GPs. The NHS website provides much data about the standards of the service provided by the NHS, such as trends in waiting lists. To access the website, visit www.heinemann.co.uk/hotlinks.

Chapter 4 – The main jobs in health, social care and early years services

This chapter covers what care work involves and the skills and qualities that care practitioners need to perform their work roles. It looks at the roles of direct and indirect care workers in all three areas and how changes in services and their provision affect the job roles of workers. It then goes on to look at communication skills and why it is so important that care workers have them, as well as the different communication needs of the client groups using the services.

Teaching tip

This is the area where asking speakers into school is most valuable. If you try and get speakers who cover a range of jobs from the different sectors the students will learn a lot and so will you! If a child minder is available and brings some children or babies along it all adds to the enjoyment for the students. The students get more out of the speakers if they prepare a set of questions to ask – the worksheet 'Jobs in health, social care and early years services' provided on the CD-ROM helps the students to write the questions. They can then be encouraged to write up each set of notes and produce a job file. Inviting someone from an organisation such as Childline is particularly interesting to the students and they may even decide to raise some money for the organisation, which contributes very well to the Key Skill of Working with Others.

Your LEA and local Education Business Partnership can provide contacts with various health, social care and early years services.

Suggested additional activities for students

There are various ways to liven up the communication section of this chapter.

Facial expressions and body language

Using magazines, newspapers etc., cut out a selection of pictures of people with different expressions on their faces and stick all the ones that convey, for example, frustration, on one piece of card and all the others that convey another mood or feeling on another until you have at least 20 cards. Number each one and put them in separate plastic wallets. The students can come and take one at a time and write down what the one word is that is conveyed by that one card. It is time consuming but once it is done it is done. You could also do this with cartoon faces on card. The students can then be asked to bring in five pictures from home that convey something to them and share them with the rest of the group.

Body language

The students can be asked to produce a freeze frame showing how they would use body language in different situations, for example, kneeling down at the same level as a child so as not to frighten them. If you have a digital camera available in school you could photograph them and print the pictures out to go in the students' portfolios to show that they have those communication skills.

You could make a series of gestures at the students, such as thumbs up or shaking a fist, and ask them to say what they mean. It is amazing just how many there are that everyone recognises.

Listening skills

One of each pair of students could be given a picture of an object, preferably drawn in 2D so as to make it possible, and they give instructions to their partners such as 'Draw a vertical line from the top right hand corner to . . .' and their partners have to follow the instructions. They then get another picture and swap roles.

Chapter 5 – The value of bases of care work

This chapter looks at the values that care workers promote through their work and how all services are aiming at helping people to be as independent as possible. It covers the balance between action and inaction and the possible consequences of both. The Care Value Base is now not always referred to as such and it also has seven areas instead of the three from GNVQ Foundation. The chapter ends by looking at guidelines such as policies, procedures and employment contracts as well as codes of practice.

Unit 1 Assessment

The assessment for Unit 1 takes the form of an investigation into local services and some of the roles of direct care workers. The best way to collect the information for this is by inviting speakers and arranging work placements for the students. These are both covered in the introduction to this resource file. Student information sheets telling the students what they need to do can be found in the assessment part of this file, along with a work placement diary. This assignment is worth 33.3% of the final marks.

Resources

Useful organisations

Age Concern,
1268 London Road,
London SW16 4ER

Carers National Association,
20/25 Glasshouse Yard,
London EC1A 4JS

Help the Aged,
207–221 Pentonville Road
London N1 9UZ

The British Dietetic Association,
5th Floor, Charles House,
148/9 Great Charles Street, Queensway,
Birmingham B3 3HT

Useful websites

Links to 'The Patient's Charter and You' and 'Your Guide to the NHS' can be found on www.heinemann.co.uk/hotlinks

Unit 1 Student information sheet 1

THE MAJOR CLIENT GROUPS

Client group name	Age range (years)
Babies and children	0–11
Adolescents	11–18
Adults	19–65
Older people	65+
Disabled people	People of any age who are well but have special needs because of a physical or mental disability

AN OVERVIEW OF HEALTH AND SOCIAL CARE PROVISION

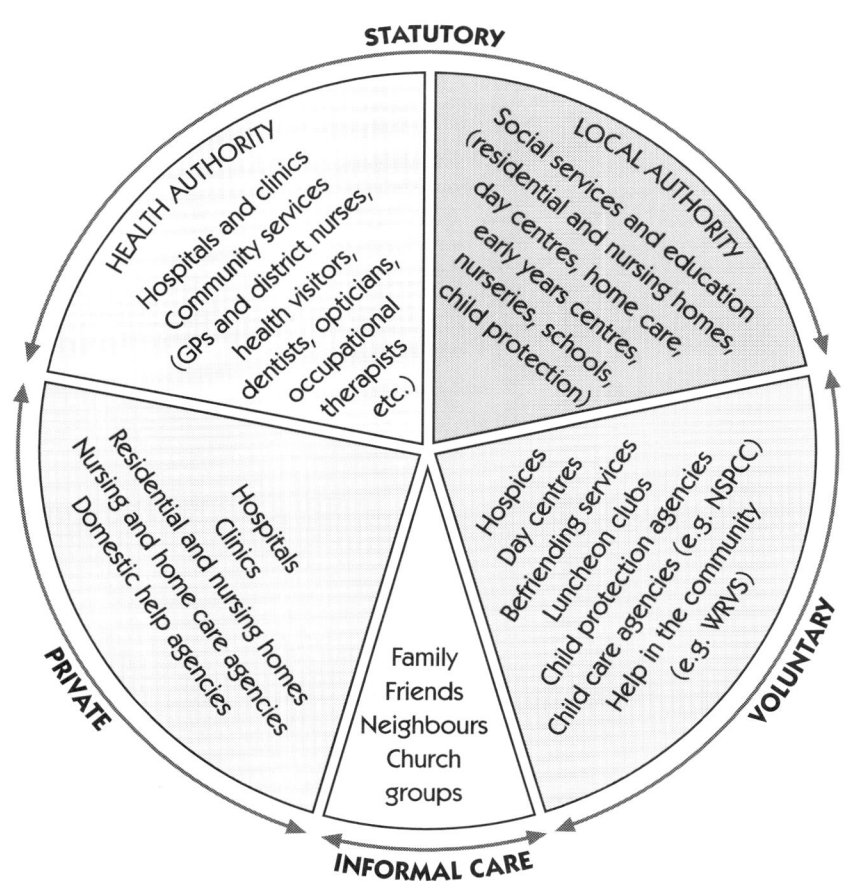

DEFINITIONS OF STATUTORY AND NON-STATUTORY SERVICES

Statutory

These are the services which health, social care and education sectors have a duty by law to provide.

Non-statutory

These are services provided by people and organisations who do not have a duty by law to provide. These are:

- *Voluntary*: services provided by people who are not paid for the care work they do, although the organisers may be paid.

- *Independent (private)*: services provided by care organisations which are run as businesses. Therefore, there must be profit in order to pay for staff, facilities and premises.

Unit 1 Student information sheet 3

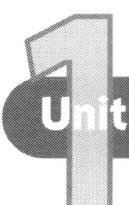

THE HEALTH CARE STRUCTURE OF ENGLAND, WALES, SCOTLAND AND NORTHERN IRELAND

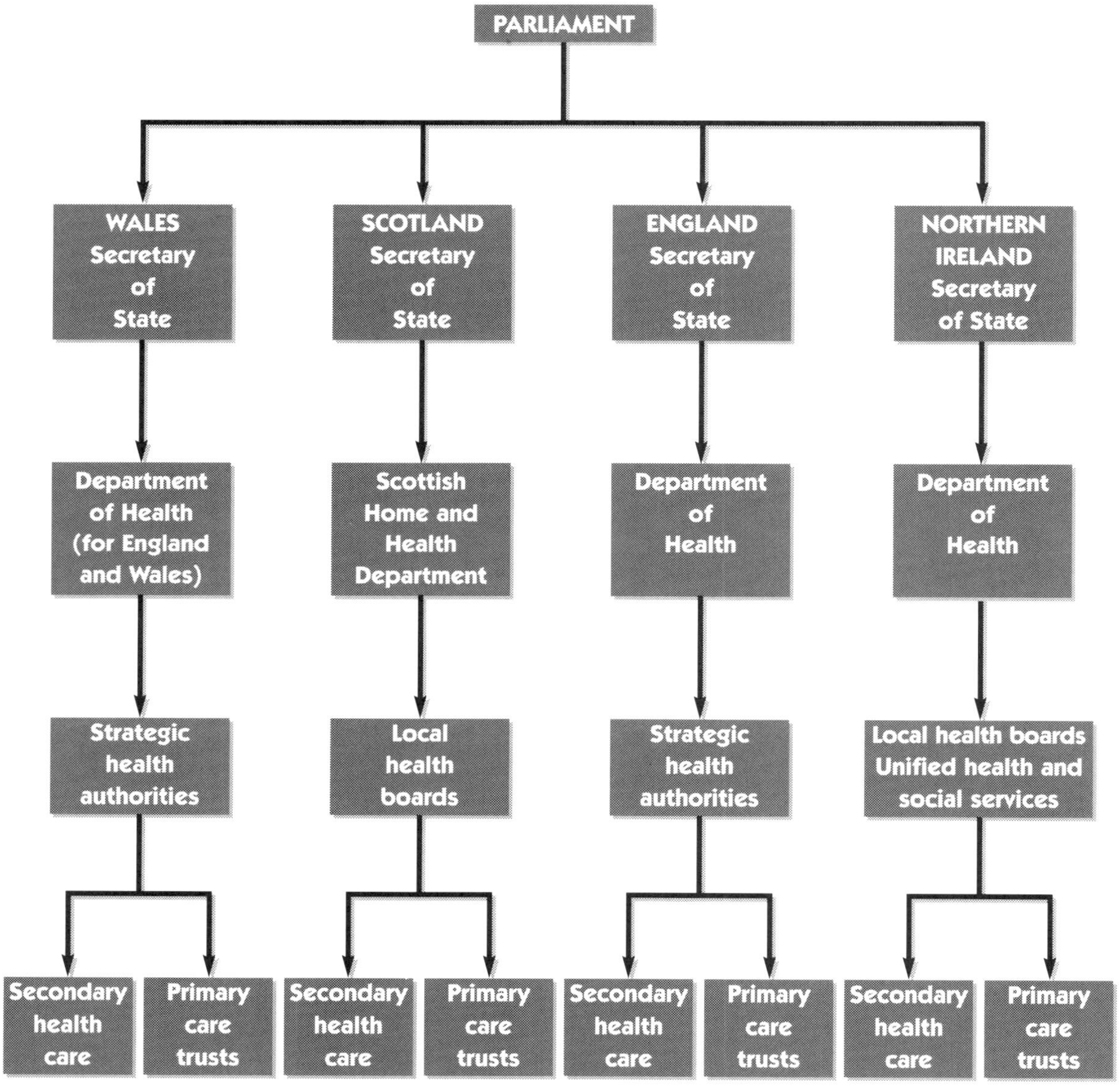
PARLIAMENT
WALES Secretary of State
SCOTLAND Secretary of State
ENGLAND Secretary of State
NORTHERN IRELAND Secretary of State
Department of Health (for England and Wales)
Scottish Home and Health Department
Department of Health
Department of Health
Strategic health authorities
Local health boards
Strategic health authorities
Local health boards Unified health and social services
Secondary health care
Primary care trusts
Secondary health care
Primary care trusts
Secondary health care
Primary care trusts
Secondary health care
Primary care trusts

Unit 1 Student information sheet 4

DIFFERENT SOCIAL CARE FUNCTIONS

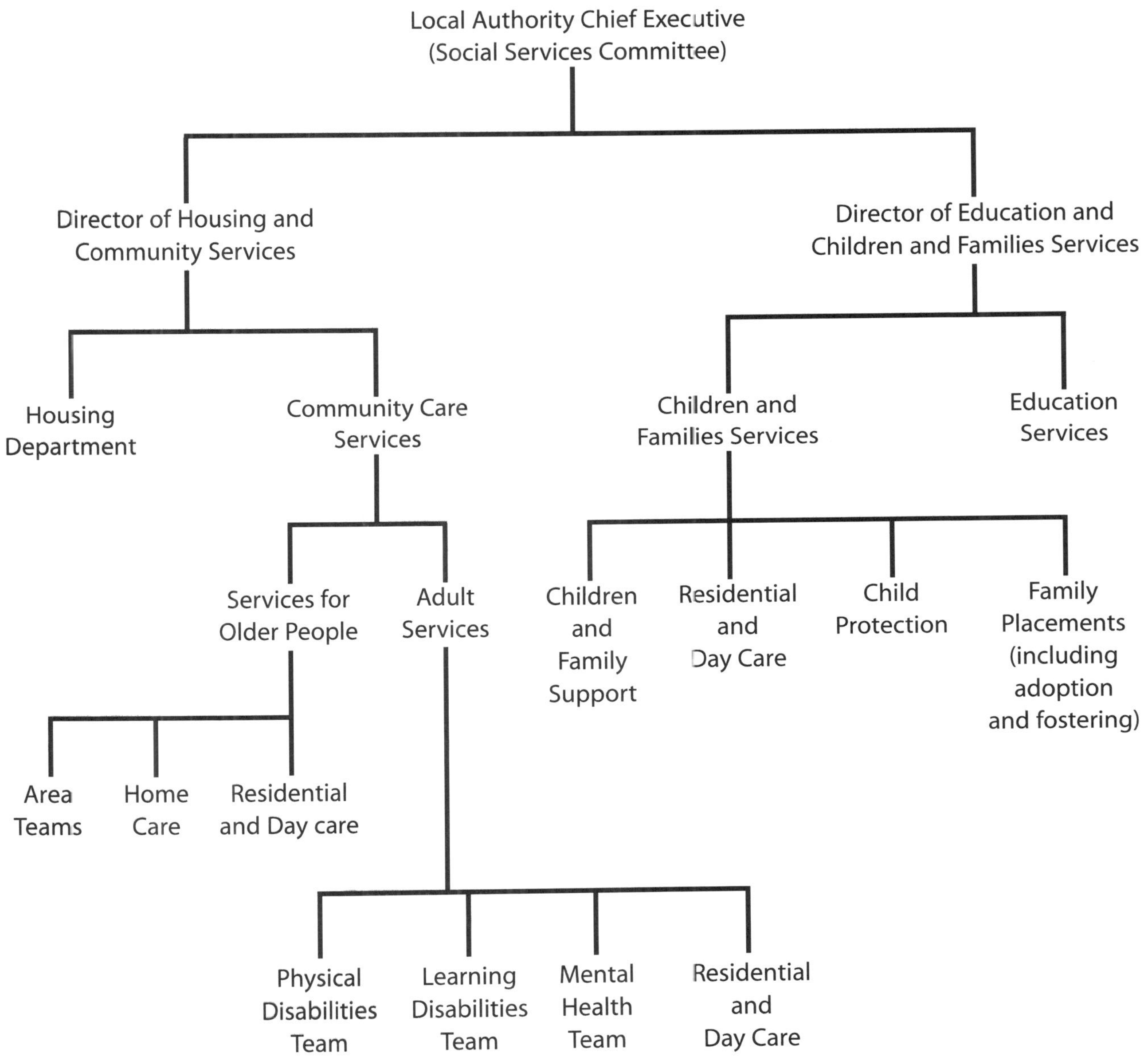

Local Authority Chief Executive
(Social Services Committee)

Director of Housing and
Community Services

Director of Education and
Children and Families Services

Housing
Department

Community Care
Services

Children and
Families Services

Education
Services

Services for
Older People

Adult
Services

Children
and
Family
Support

Residential
and
Day Care

Child
Protection

Family
Placements
(including
adoption
and fostering)

Area
Teams

Home
Care

Residential
and Day care

Physical
Disabilities
Team

Learning
Disabilities
Team

Mental
Health
Team

Residential
and
Day Care

Unit 1 Student information sheet 5

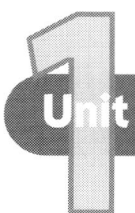

TASKS OF THE GENERAL SOCIAL CARE COUNCIL

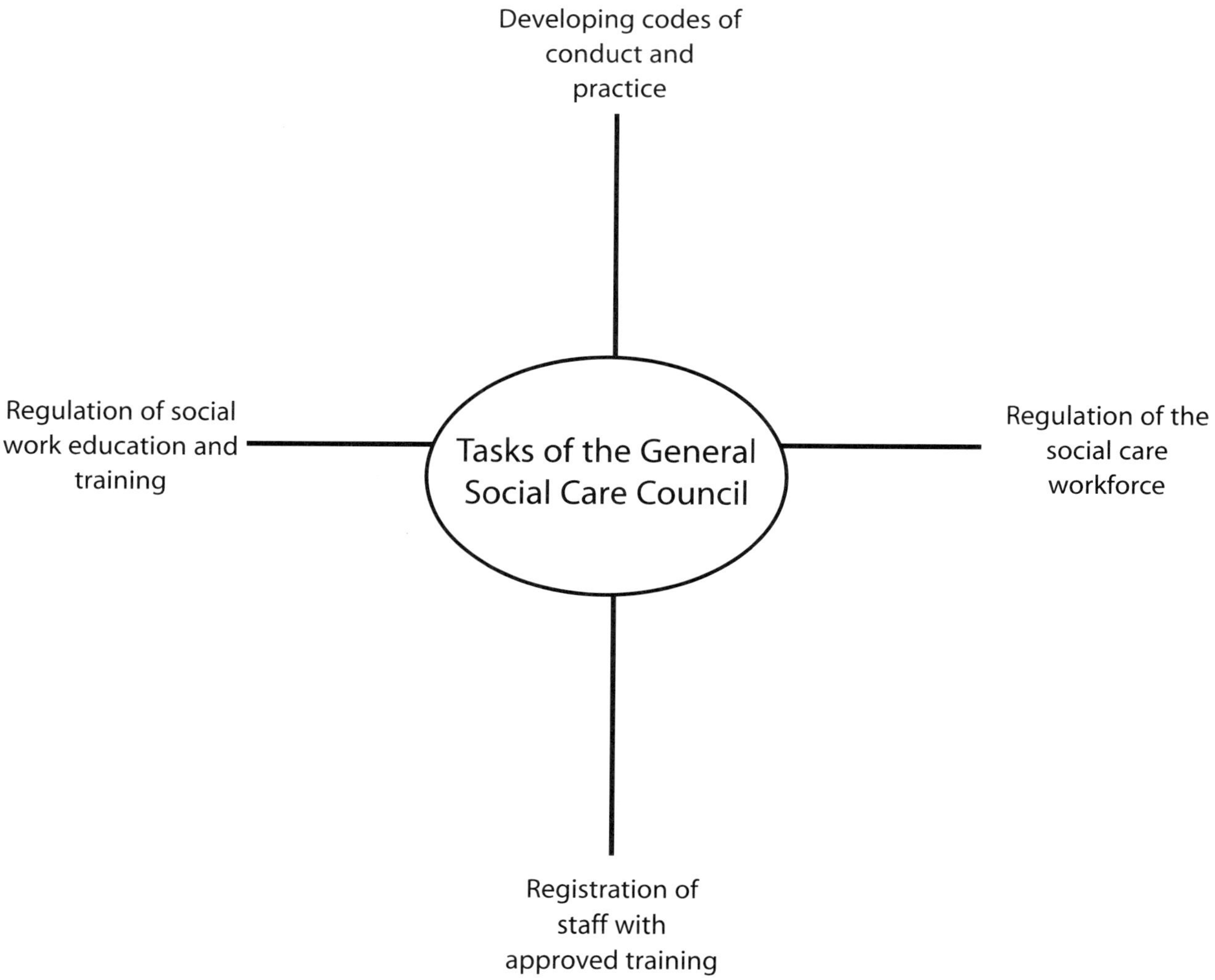
Developing codes of conduct and practice
Regulation of social work education and training
Tasks of the General Social Care Council
Regulation of the social care workforce
Registration of staff with approved training

Physical barriers
Stairs, a lack of lifts and a lack of adapted toilet facilities can prevent access by people with mobility problems.

Cultural and language barriers
Cultural beliefs about who should provide care and how illness and social problems should be dealt with, as well as difficulties in using English, may deter members of some communities from using care services.

Psychological barriers
Fear of losing independence, the stigma associated with some services and not wanting to be looked after can deter people from making use of care services. Mental health problems can also prevent those in need from accessing services.

BARRIERS TO CARE

Resource barriers
Lack of staff, lack of information about services, lack of money to fund services or a large demand for services can prevent people from gaining access to services when they need or want them.

Financial barriers
Charges and fees can deter and exclude people who have not got the money to pay for the services they need.

Geographical barriers
In rural areas the location of an organisation or practitioner may be a barrier to use if there is also a lack of public transport or a long bus or car journey is required to get there.

1. Promoting anti-discriminatory practice
   - Freedom from discrimination
   - The right to be different
   - Aware of assumptions made surrounding gender, race, age, sexuality, disability and class
   - Understand prejudice, stereotyping and labelling and their effects
   - Use of language (political correctness)

2. Maintaining confidentiality of information
   - Secure recording systems
   - The need and right to know
   - Value and protect client
   - Policies, procedures and guidelines
   - Boundaries and tensions in maintaining confidentiality

3. Promoting and supporting individuals' rights
   - Dignity
   - Independence
   - Health
   - Safety
   - Choice
   - Effective communication

4. Acknowledging individuals' personal beliefs and identity
   - The benefits of diversity
   - Choice
   - Respect
   - The right to be different

CARE WORKERS EMPOWER CLIENTS BY

5. Protecting individuals from abuse
   - Hostile or negative feelings
   - Support
   - Dignity

6. Promoting effective communication and relationships
   - Provide and obtain information
   - Express values
   - Express and understand needs, fears and wishes
   - Maintain identity

7. Providing individualised care
   - Control of own life
   - Respect
   - Needs catered for
   - Improve quality of life
   - Provide independence
   - Balance between control and assistance

Find out what the Youth Service and the Youth Offending Services are and what services they provide in your local area. You can do this by contacting agencies such as social services or by using the Internet or library.

The Youth Service is:

_____

_____

_____

The Youth Service provides the following services in this area:

_____

_____

_____

The Youth Offending Services are:

_____

_____

_____

The Youth Offending Services provide the following services in this area:

_____

_____

_____

_____

Extension activity

▷ Split into two groups. Decide which group is to do task one and which is to do task two. You will need an action plan sheet to complete the tasks.

Task one
If you have a young offenders' detention centre or a prison near your school, contact them and ask if a member of staff from there would be able either to come along to talk to your class about the service they provide or send some information for your group to report back to the class.

Task two
Find out who the child protection officer is in school – every school has to have one. Arrange for that person to come along to one of your lessons if possible to talk to the whole class about the laws and set procedures concerned with child protection. If that is not possible, make an appointment to speak to that person at their convenience. Report back to the rest of the class.

Case study

Rashid is 52 years old and has lost his managerial job. He has never been out of work before and does not know how to go about applying for benefits. He has also never been to a job centre before and is very apprehensive about going. He is depressed because he suspects he was chosen as one of the managers to be made redundant because his recently appointed boss might be racist. She has never said anything directly to him but he has always felt that she doesn't like him. Rashid was born and educated in the UK. He has often heard his manager complain about illegal immigrants coming into the country and taking jobs that white people should have. He does not know whether he should take her to a tribunal for unfair dismissal.

He is also depressed because he feels it is his role to support his family but now they are relying on his wife's earnings from her part-time job. He feels he is letting the family down and that he is too old to have a chance of another job, having been with the same company all his working life. His daughter is due to get married next year which is another worry as she wants a big wedding and he has said he would pay for most of it. He starts to have headaches and feels numb down the side of his face and is reluctant to go out in the evening as he feels guilty spending money on beer.

1. What services can Rashid call upon to help him with:

   • Coping with being redundant? _____

   _____

   • Applying for benefits? _____

   _____

   • Getting another job? _____

   _____

   • His suspicion that he has been unfairly dismissed? _____

   _____

   • His depression? _____

2. Imagine that Rashid lives in your area. How can he find out about these services?

   _____

   _____

   _____

   _____

   _____

3. How have Rashid's needs been affected by him losing his job:

- Health? _____

  _____

- Developmental? _____

  _____

- Social? _____

  _____

- Emotional? _____

  _____

Extension activity

▷ Do some research on the subject of unfair dismissal in relation to issues of race. Write a short summary of what you find out to share with the rest of the class.

Unit **Policy making**

1. In a group choose one rule that you have in your school that you do not think is fair. Write it down:

_____

2. Discuss why the school has that rule. List the reasons below.

_____

_____

_____

3. Discuss whether you would have come up with the same rule if your group was in charge and had the authority to decide on the school rules. Yes / No

4. Would you be more likely to stick to the rule if you had been involved in discussions about it before it was imposed (forced) on you? Yes / No

5. Write down the reasons for your answer:

_____

_____

_____

6. Why would involving young people in drawing up a policy help improve the process and make the policy more likely to work?

_____

_____

_____

Extension activity

▷ In a group discuss the government policy on introducing more speed cameras but painting them in a bright colour so that drivers can see them and slow down. Do you think that people will be more likely to take note and slow down because the government has been honest with people and told them they will be there or do you think that they should have just put more grey ones up so that they catch more people speeding? Write the arguments for and against painting them in bright colours below:

Yes because:	No because:

Unit Social policy goals

The Government has set a target to reduce the number of children aged 11 – 15 who smoke regularly from 13 per cent in 1996 to 11 per cent by 2005, and 9 per cent or less by 2010. This is an example of a **social policy goal.**

Percentage of students who were regular smokers (i.e smoking at least one cigarette a week on average), 1982 to 2000												
Age in years	1982	1984	1986	1988	1990	1992	1994	1996	1998	1999	2000	Average
11	0	0	0	0	0	0	1	0	1	1	1	
12	2	2	2	1	2	2	2	3	3	3	2	
13	7	10	5	5	7	7	6	9	7	6	8	
14	16	17	11	10	13	14	17	18	17	12	15	
15	25	28	22	20	25	23	28	30	24	23	23	
Total	11	13	10	8	10	10	12	13	11	9	10	

1. Complete the last column of the table by working out the average percentage for each age group. To do this you need to add up all the figures on a particular line and divide by 11. Compare the figures for 2000 with your average column. Do you think there has been much change in smoking habits between 1982 and 2000? Explain your answer.

2. Compare the figures for 1996, the baseline the Government started with, and the figures for 2000. Which age groups, if any, have:

    *   stayed much the same? _____

    *   increased? _____

    *   decreased? _____

3. Do you think the Government has made any progress towards its goal? If so, who with?

    _____

4. Draw a bar chart on the back of this worksheet showing age against percentage of smokers for 2000. At which age is there the biggest increase in the numbers smoking?

    _____

5. What do you suggest the Government does to target these young people?

    _____

Contact your local library or Primary Care Trust and ask them for a copy of a summary of the main points of the Health Improvement Plan. Do not attempt to read the actual plan – it is very long and complex – unless you really want to of course!

1. Write down each of the main targets or goals as bullet points on the back of this worksheet.

2. Try to find out how the authors collected the information in order to identify what needs improving:

   • Who did they ask? _____

   • How many people did they ask? _____

3. Look at the main targets. From your experience of doctors, hospitals, walk-in-centres etc. do you agree that the areas identified need improving? Explain your answer.

   _____

   _____

   _____

   _____

   _____

4. Is there anything that hasn't been identified that you feel needs improving? If you can't think of anything, discuss it with others in the group or your family.

   _____

   _____

Extension activity

▷ Write a polite but firm letter to the authors to tell them what you think needs improving and why. Ask them what they are doing about the problem.

Why people use health, social care and early years services

Case study

Ben and Cindy have just discovered that they are expecting their first child in four months. They have no home of their own, so they are living with Cindy's parents, who are very worried about the situation, as they have no physical space. They are already caring for Grandad who is a wheelchair user and is confused most of the time. Cindy's mother is constantly tired out and exhausted.

Ben and Cindy have done nothing but fight since they moved into the family house. They have little privacy and no money as Ben has still not found employment.

Ben has started drinking too much alcohol as a way of coping with the stresses and strains of the situation but this is making things worse from Cindy's point of view.

Make a list below of the kind of help and services you would recommend for Ben, Cindy, Grandad and Cindy's parents.

Give your reasons for recommending the service and explain how you think the service can support the family member.

Client	Help and services	Reasons for support
Ben		
Cindy		
Grandad		
Cindy's parents		

Unit 1 Local statutory services

Use either Chapter 2 of the GCSE Health and Social Care textbook, or ask a speaker if one is arranged from, for example, the local Primary Care Trust, to find three statutory services available in your area, which would help to meet the needs of each of the clients listed below. Complete the table with all the information asked for.

Client	Name of service	Primary, secondary or tertiary care?	Details of service provided
A baby			
A 7 year old girl			
A pregnant teenager			
A man with learning difficulties			
A elderly woman partially paralysed by a stroke			

Extension activity

▷ Pick one of the services mentioned above in agreement with your teacher and do some research into it, so that you can prepare a 5-minute presentation on it. Include an image generated by a computer or on an overhead transparency. Produce a handout containing a brief outline of the key points about the service for each member of your class. You could do this in the form of a mind map.

Unit 1 Voluntary organisations

In a group, find out about support groups and voluntary organisations in your area. They should cover the full range of health, social care and early years services. Discuss how you are going to tackle the task to cover as many groups as you can. Complete the table below for the groups that you personally are given to investigate. Then present the information in an attractive way using a computer, so that it can be printed off for other members of the class.

	Health Care	Social Care	Early Years
Name			
Logo (symbol)			
What they do i.e. what services they provide			
How they are funded			
Where they are based			
Who their clients are			
Any other notes			

Extension activity

▷ Pick one of the organisations and try to find out:

- who set up the service _____
- why they set it up _____
- what training the workers need _____
- what qualities the workers need _____
- what the benefits are of having such an organisation in your area _____

To do this really well, if time permits, you could ring the head office of the organisation and arrange to interview someone. You could tape the interview but you must ask permission first.

In the table below you will find a list of personal needs for an elderly client who wants to live at home because he treasures his independence but needs help to do so. Write down the type of carer who could help with a particular need and who would provide the service. The first one is done for you.

Personal needs	Type of carer	Service provider
• Bathing, toileting, personal hygiene	Home care assistant (direct carer)	Social services
• Daily housework		
• Shopping		
Clinical needs		
• Wound dressing		
• Giving particular medication		
Needs to adapt the home		
• Hoists and bath aids		
• Aids for mobility		
• Aids to help with dressing, housework, cooking and eating		
Respite needs for carers and clients		
• Short-term respite (just a few hours)		
• Longer term (parts of week or week)		

Extension activity

▷ Collect leaflets from places such as social services and the library and cut out adverts from magazines and newspapers that show the range of help on offer and the variety of aids to help in the home that are available, such as walk-in baths.

Unit 1 Psychological barriers to care

Case study

Jayshree lives alone in a sheltered home unit. She has many friends around her, but is increasingly worried about using the shops or going to the doctor or to the library where she enjoys spending time. Her main problem is that she had an operation on her throat recently and she can't speak very loudly. She hates it when people say 'pardon' all the time. She recently had a letter from the doctor asking her to go for a check up, but she simply couldn't face the journey.

1. What kind of barrier(s) may be preventing Jayshree from using her local services?

    _____

    _____

    _____

    _____

    _____

    _____

2. What other care services might Jayshree have difficulty in accessing and why?

    _____

    _____

    _____

    _____

    _____

    _____

3. If you were living near Jayshree, how could you help her, or advise her, to make her access to care easier?

    _____

    _____

    _____

    _____

    _____

    _____

    _____

Imagine that your group is a committee which has to decide whether to pay for a little girl to have a life saving heart transplant, a number of elderly patients to have hip replacements so that they can walk without pain again or a dialysis machine which will keep several people alive while they are waiting for a kidney transplant.

Appoint a chairperson and discuss the problem. The group can only afford one of the three alternatives and the majority of the group has to agree with the decision taken. Your group will have to explain their reasons for the decision at the end of the discussion so you will need to appoint someone to take notes and feed back to the other groups.

Decision made: _____

Reasons:

_____

_____

_____

_____

Extension activity

1. How do you feel about people who have to make decisions like this as part of their day-to-day work?

   _____

   _____

   _____

2. How easy was it to make a decision?

   _____

   _____

3. If this was a real life situation you might receive letters and phone calls from relatives trying to influence your decision or criticising your decision once it was made. How would that make you feel?

   _____

   _____

4. As a result of your group's decision someone will die but others will live. How do you feel about people who have to make such decisions now that you have had a go at doing it yourself?

   _____

   _____

   _____

   _____

Anytown Social Services Department has recently had approval to carry out some work on its building. It is an old building, spacious inside, but certainly needs a facelift and improvement in facilities. The following improvements have been suggested. Can you add beside them what barriers these improvements would remove, and who might benefit from them? The first has been started for you.

Improvement	Barrier removed	Benefit
An all-weather ramp up to the main entrance	*Physical*	*Wheelchair user*
Automatic opening doors		
Information in locally used languages about all services		
Staff available for longer hours		
New coat of paint		
Crèche facilities		
New lifts with lower operating panels		
Staff training in communication skills		
Suggestion box at reception area		
Information about what to do out of hours		
Canteen for light refreshments		

CASH PRESSURE FORCES OLD TO LEAVE WARD BEDS

Thousands of sick pensioners are having to leave their hospital beds early to avoid pension cuts. Older patients who stay in hospital longer than six weeks have their state pensions cut by £28.50 a week, Age Concern has revealed. The Government claims that they are not paying rent while they are in hospital but in fact they continue to pay and so come out of hospital before they are better because they are frightened about losing money. In September 2000, 31,500 pensioners were facing a possible pension reduction.

---

1. Read the newspaper cutting.

2. What kinds of barriers to care are preventing the pensioners concerned having full access to the services which they need?

_____

_____

3. Why are pensioners being pressurised to leave hospital early?

_____

_____

_____

_____

4. How many pensioners were facing a pension reduction in September 2000?

_____

5. As a potential worker in the health and social care area, what is your opinion on whether pensioners should have their benefits cut if they are in hospital for more than six weeks?

_____

_____

_____

_____

_____

_____

Extension activity

▷ Find out the name of your local MP. Write a letter to your MP either giving your support or objecting to the rule of pensioners having their pensions cut if they are in hospital longer than six weeks. Give your reasons why, including the possible effects on the health and well-being of pensioners. Format your letter out properly and word process it if possible.

Case study

Mary works part-time as a carer for a voluntary organisation. She visits people who are in need of home help with another full-time carer. She mostly looks after Mr Potts, who is a single man with limited mobility, and Fran Sharrock, a woman who has recently had a stroke. One of Mary's tasks is to find out what shopping they require each week and then go to purchase the items. She can complete this task very quickly with Mr Potts but is experiencing difficulties communicating with Fran.

Facts about strokes
A person who has a stroke has a loss of brain function caused by lack of oxygen and death of tissue in some part of the brain. Symptoms vary according to the part of the brain affected. Common symptoms are paralysis of part of the body, weakness, loss of coordination, vision difficulties and difficulty speaking.

1. Fran has all the symptoms mentioned above. Suggest which of these has led to Mary having difficulty communicating with Fran.

   _____

   _____

   _____

   _____

   _____

2. Suggest ways in which Mary can try to overcome these problems.

   _____

   _____

   _____

   _____

   _____

   _____

3. Name the types of communication you have suggested in each part of your answer to question 2.

_____

_____

_____

_____

_____

_____

4. Work in a group of three. Role-play the ways in which you would try to communicate with Fran with a partner. The third member of your group can say how effective the different methods you try are.

Extension activity

 Find out what support is available for stroke victims. Use the Internet and collect leaflets that show carers how to overcome communication difficulties.

Unit 1 — Different communication needs of children

Case study

Thomas is eight years old and he has been asked to leave his primary school because his behaviour is aggressive and unpredictable, so much so that he poses a threat to other children. The final straw was when he threw a stone at another child and it hit him on the head, narrowly avoiding his eye and cutting his skin so that the child is now scarred. This was not the first time he had thrown stones at other children and he had been told of the dangers of such behaviour. He is now being sent to a behavioural support unit during the day but does not understand why he has to go. You are his newly appointed social worker and it is your job to explain to him why he has to attend such a unit, without upsetting him.

1. Think carefully about what you would say to him. Make notes below.

   _____

   _____

   _____

   _____

2. What other communication methods would you use?

   _____

   _____

   _____

3. Where you would tell him?

   _____

4. How would you position yourself?

   _____

5. What you would do if he started to get upset?

   _____

   _____

Extension activity

▷ With a partner, role-play the situation with Thomas, first in a way which you feel demonstrates poor communication skills and then again, but this time demonstrating effective communication skills. You might be asked to show it to the rest of your class. They can suggest ways in which you could have done even better, if possible.

If you have access to a video camera ask someone in your group to record the role plays so that the class can refer to parts of the tape in the discussion on how to improve the communication skills still further.

Unit 1 Different communication needs of disabled people

Case study

Cedric has been in a psychiatric hospital for fifteen years and is now preparing to live in the community again. He has to learn how to catch a bus on his own. Imagine he is going to live near your school. Write down what you would say to him, if you were his care worker, if you were trying to teach him how to catch a bus to the next town to you. Remember that he will not know much about money and has only been on a bus a couple of times in the last few years, always accompanied by a care worker.

Points I would need to make:

_____

_____

_____

_____

_____

_____

_____

_____

_____

Other things I would have to consider:

_____

_____

_____

_____

_____

_____

Extension activity

▷ Imagine you are Cedric and have been taught in the way you have just suggested in your notes above. Write down how Cedric might be feeling about the experience of learning to travel on a bus to the nearest town on his own.

_____

_____

_____

_____

Unit 1 · The balance between action and inaction

Case study

Natasha and Ed have already got two boys, aged 14 and 15, and have always wanted a girl to complete their family. Natasha has been unable to conceive and they are too old to adopt a child so they decide to buy a baby girl from another country in response to an advertisement on the Internet. The natural parents are poor and feel that their child would have a better life in England. The baby arrives and the family is very happy for a few months. Then Social Services hear about this and they are very concerned so take the child into care whilst they investigate. There is a lot of publicity in the newspapers and on television. The natural parents then decide that they have made a mistake and want the baby returned. Natasha and Ed go to court to try to get the baby they bought back but in the end the baby is returned to its real parents. Natasha and Ed are heart broken and argue that if Social Services had not got involved they would still have the baby and the baby would have a better life because they have a nice home and plenty of money.

1. Try to write down all the reasons why the Social Services were right to take action.

_____

_____

_____

_____

_____

2. Write down any reasons you can think of to support the couple that bought the baby.

_____

_____

_____

_____

_____

3. How do you think the two boys will have been affected by the situation?

_____

_____

_____

_____

_____

4. In a group, discuss the reasons for and against the Social Services becoming involved. Try to decide as a group whether Social Services were right to get involved. Give the main reason for the group's decision.

_____

_____

_____

_____

_____

Extension activity

▷ Prepare a role-play based on the situation in the activity above. Decide what you think is motivating each of the parties concerned. Perform the role-play for the rest of the class. Try to convey how the family, the care workers and the natural mother feel at each stage of the situation.

Unit 1 Promoting anti-discriminatory practice

Be really honest with yourself in this activity. You don't need to show your answers to anyone else.

1. Look at Figure 5.2 on page 69 of the GCSE Health and Social Care textbook showing the dangers of discrimination and write down a description of yourself using each of the headings.

    _____

    _____

    _____

    _____

2. Now try to work out what dangers of discrimination exist for you. For example, you may have put under the heading under health that you are overweight. This may make you feel as though others make fun of you behind your back.

    _____

    _____

    _____

3. Which group/s of people are most likely to discriminate against you?

    _____

    _____

4. What groups of people are you likely to make assumptions about, even though you might not express these assumptions to other people?

    _____

    _____

5. Do you ever express these assumptions to other people? If so, to whom?

    _____

6. Can you think of any occasion when you have made a comment about someone because you see that person as different from yourself? Do you say it so that they could hear?

    _____

7. How do you think that will have made them feel?

    _____

8. Now you have thought through each of these questions make a resolution about how you intend to treat those you see as different from yourself in a more positive and supportive way and stick to it. Set yourself a target (write it on the back of this sheet) and ask a close friend to help you stick to it if you want to. You will need to be able to do this if you are to become a care worker.

Have a group discussion based on the following questions.

1. Why do you think there are so few male nurses, childminders and nursery teachers?

_____

_____

2. Why do you think there are so few females in positions such as Cabinet Ministers or airline pilots?

_____

_____

3. Are there any males working in your school kitchens? If not, why do you think this is?

_____

_____

4. Are the heads of department and the head and deputy heads in your school mainly male or female? Why do you think this is?

_____

_____

5. In answering these questions, have you made any judgements about people because of their gender or put a certain viewpoint because of your own gender? Be honest!

_____

_____

6. Can you think of any factors which might stop a male or female being promoted as far as they should be because of their gender?

_____

_____

At the end of the discussion try to decide on a definition of stereotyping without looking in a dictionary. Check your answer with your teacher.

_____

_____

Extension activity

▷ 1. Try to explain the difference between prejudice and discrimination by filling the gaps in the following sentence:

Prejudice is what a person .... whilst discrimination is what a person
....

2. Try to find out what the proper names are for the following forms of discrimination:

age _____, gender _____, race _____ and sexual orientation _____.

(Hint: some of them end in ...ism, others in ...obia!)

Unit 1 Written communication

Case study

Catherine is 66 years old and has severe arthritis. She is no longer able to get in and out of the bath and keeps burning herself when she makes a cup of tea because the stiffness in her fingers makes it hard for her to pour water out of the kettle without spilling some on herself.

Imagine you are a community nurse who visits Catherine and is becoming concerned for her safety and worried that she can no longer look after herself properly. Write a letter to social services enquiring about the options available, such as a live-in home help, sheltered accommodation or a residential home. Structure your letter properly and think about the language you use – this would be more formal than the sort of informal letter you might write to a friend.

Extension activity

▷ Write a report on Catherine to accompany your letter to social services. It should be a record of the details of several of your visits to Catherine.

If you are told a secret and it has been told to you in confidence, you should keep it confidential. The table below gives three examples of information and the consequences of not keeping it confidential. Think of others – they can be about school or life in general – and complete the table.

Information	Consequences of not keeping it confidential
You know when someone's home is going to be unoccupied for a period of time because of a family holiday	The person you tell might tell someone else who might be tempted to break in
You tell a friend what you feel about something personal	You won't tell that friend how you feel about anything personal again
You are in a residential home and tell your carer something which he promises not to repeat	Your self-esteem goes down, you don't feel valued or respected and you won't tell your carer something private again

Unit 1 Maintaining confidentiality (continued)

Extension activity

▷ Take one of the situations from the table above. Role play it in a small group so that when you show it to the rest of the group the seriousness of breaking a confidence is made very clear.

Can you think of situations when you think it would be right to break a confidence?

_____

_____

_____

_____

_____

_____

_____

_____

Unit 2 — Promoting health and well-being

Overview

This unit is a good one to start with as many of the topics are ones that students have come across before, either in PSHE or other subjects, and are also the types of issues that already affect them in their own lives. There is plenty of opportunity for debate as students are naturally interested in these issues.

Chapter 6 – Understanding health and well-being

This chapter looks at the different ways of thinking about health and well-being and the way ideas have changed over time and between different cultures.

Teaching tip

Leaflets are available from associations such as Age Concern on how older people can keep warm and how their other needs can be met. The Department of Health produce booklets such as 'Health and well-being: a guide for older people,' which contain many useful addresses. Such leaflets will be useful if the individual chosen for the assignment is an older person.

Activity

Ask students to cut pictures out of magazines and catalogues of babies with various types of toys, being cuddled by an adult, being pushed in a pram etc. By sticking the pictures on four pieces of card, students can illustrate the physical, intellectual, emotional and social needs of babies easily and in a way that is readily accessible to all abilities. The students can then find pictures for other client groups.

Chapter 7 – Factors positively influencing health and well-being

This chapter looks at the way a person's health and well-being is affected by different factors throughout the lifespan. For those who have taught GNVQ Foundation, please note that Social Class is no longer mentioned as a factor but supportive relationships, the use of health monitoring and illness prevention services and risk management techniques are additional factors.

Teaching tip

There are many leaflets around that help with this chapter. For example, the big supermarket chains produce leaflets on a wide range of health-related topics such as diets for those with diabetes and so on. There are also numerous leaflets on health monitoring and illness prevention available from the Department of Health.

Activity

Arrange a trip to a local leisure facility and get the students to do some physical exercise under supervision. You could also invite the manager of your local gym to come and speak to the students about the health and fitness industry. This activity not only helps them to become health wise but they get to see the business side of health and fitness.

Chapter 8 – Risks to health and well-being

This chapter covers the factors that are a risk to health and well-being and their damaging effect. New factors have been introduced such as genetically inherited diseases, social isolation and environmental pollution. The chapter goes on to consider factors over which people have a degree of control as well as those that they are powerless to change.

Teaching tip

There is a wealth of free material available in the form of booklets and leaflets that will help in this chapter. Some examples are:

- The Issues series, published by Independence Educational Publishers, cover many of the issues in this chapter, and include topics such as alcohol, sexual health, drug abuse in sport, poverty, stress etc. They are a useful resource to provide topics for extension activity debates

- The leaflets 'A parent's guide to drugs and alcohol,' 'Think about drink,' 'Smoking: the facts' and 'The facts about HIV and AIDS' by the Health Education Authority and 'Smoking, giving up for life' by the NHS are examples of very useful informative leaflets

- 'Being Yourself' is a teenage pregnancy prevention pack, produced by Life Education International, and comes with a video

- There are also many useful health websites such as which can be found at www.heinemann.co.uk/hotlinks.

Activity

One way to introduce the 'Risks to health' section is to have a carrier bag containing the following items:

- a razor
- glue
- packet of cigarettes
- a syringe
- an aerosol can
- a condom
- some tin foil
- some paracetamol
- a needle disposal box
- a beer bottle
- a teaspoon
- some contraceptive pills
- a leaflet on sexually transmitted diseases
- anything else that can pose a risk to health, through its consumption or its use with other things.

As each one is pulled out of the bag at random, the group can discuss its use and the risks involved.

Chapter 9 – Indicators of physical health

This chapter looks at ways in which an individual's physical health can be monitored using measures such as:

- blood pressure meter
- peak flow meter

- Body Mass Index
- resting pulse and recovery after exercise.

The chapter also considers how a person's age, sex and lifestyle affect these.

Teaching tip

Your local medical centre may be able to provide photocopies of charts to record peak flow measurement on which you can use to show to the students.

Activity

Items needed to measure the indicators of physical health can be purchased from school suppliers or borrowed from the science department. Useful items include:

- A blood pressure cuff and meter
- A number of peak flow meters (with removable mouth pieces so that they can be immersed in disinfectant between each use)
- Peak flow charts, which come with the peak flow meter and can be photocopied
- Bathroom scales that measure in kilograms
- Pulse rate monitors
- A height measure in metres
- Digital timers.

Chapter 10 – Health promotion and improvement methods

This chapter covers how individuals can be motivated and supported to improve their health. It looks at how physical health assessment and target setting can be used to produce a health improvement plan for an individual and how different health behaviours can help people achieve their targets. Different types of health promotion materials are covered, and how they can inform, motivate and support people to improve their health and well-being.

Activity

Drawing up a health plan as a table on a piece of sugar paper is a useful teaching tool. The students can see how clear and accessible the information is and can then produce their own on a smaller scale.

Unit 2 Assessment

This unit is assessed by each student producing a health improvement plan for an individual of their choice. Worksheet 2.10 can be used to help them choose the individual and there is guidance on how to write a health plan on pages 141–43 of this file.

Resources

Useful addresses

Alcohol Concern,
Waterbridge House,
32–36 Loman Street,
London SE1 0EE

Breast Cancer Care,
Kiln House,
210 New Kings Road,
London SW6 4NZ

British Heart Foundation,
14 Fitzhardinge Street,
London W1H 4DH

Department of Health,
Richmond House
79 Whitehall,
London SW1A 2NS

DrugScope,
32–36 Loman Street,
London SE1 0EE

FPA (formerly The Family Planning Association),
2–12 Pentonville Road,
London N1 9FP

Fresh Focus Smoking Cessation Team,
Beech Hill Clinic,
Beech Hall Street,
Wigan WN6 7HX

Health Development Agency,
Holborn Gate,
330 High Holborn,
London WC1V 7BA

Meningitis Research Foundation,
Midland Way, Thornbury,
Bristol BS35 2BS

QUIT,
Ground floor,
211 Old Street,
London EC1V 9NR

Tacade,
1 Hulme Place,
The Crescent,
Salford
Greater Manchester M5 4QA

The Foundation for the Study of Infant Deaths (FSID),
11–19 Artillery Row,
London SW1P 1RT

Useful websites

Links to useful health websites can be found at www.heinemann.co.uk/hotlinks.

Student information sheet 1

MASLOW'S HIERARCHY OF NEEDS

Self-
actualisation
needs
(achieving
full potential)

Self-esteem needs
(respect, including
self-respect)

Love and emotional needs
(affection from others,
being with others)

Safety and security needs
(freedom from anxiety and chaos;
stability; predictability)

Basic physical needs
(food, drink, oxygen, sleep, warmth)

Unit 2 Student information sheet 2

FOUR COMPONENTS OF HEALTH

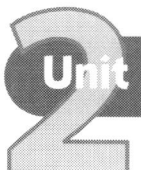

Unit 2 Student information sheet 3

FACTORS AFFECTING HEALTH AND WELL-BEING

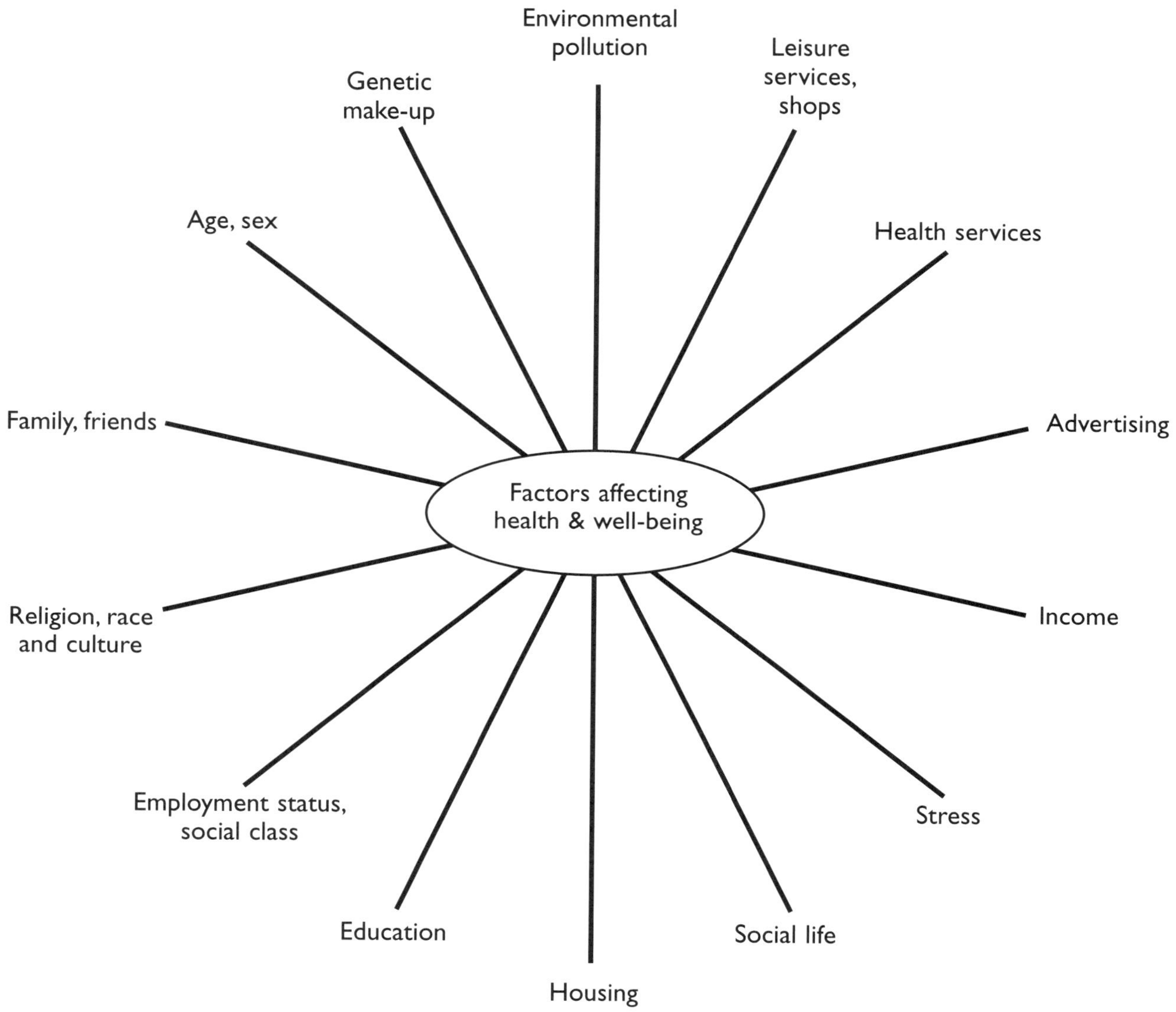

Factors affecting health & well-being
Environmental pollution
Leisure services, shops
Health services
Advertising
Income
Stress
Social life
Housing
Education
Employment status, social class
Religion, race and culture
Family, friends
Age, sex
Genetic make-up

Unit 2 Student information sheet 4

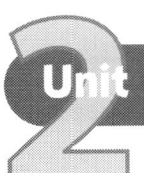

BENEFITS OF EXERCISE

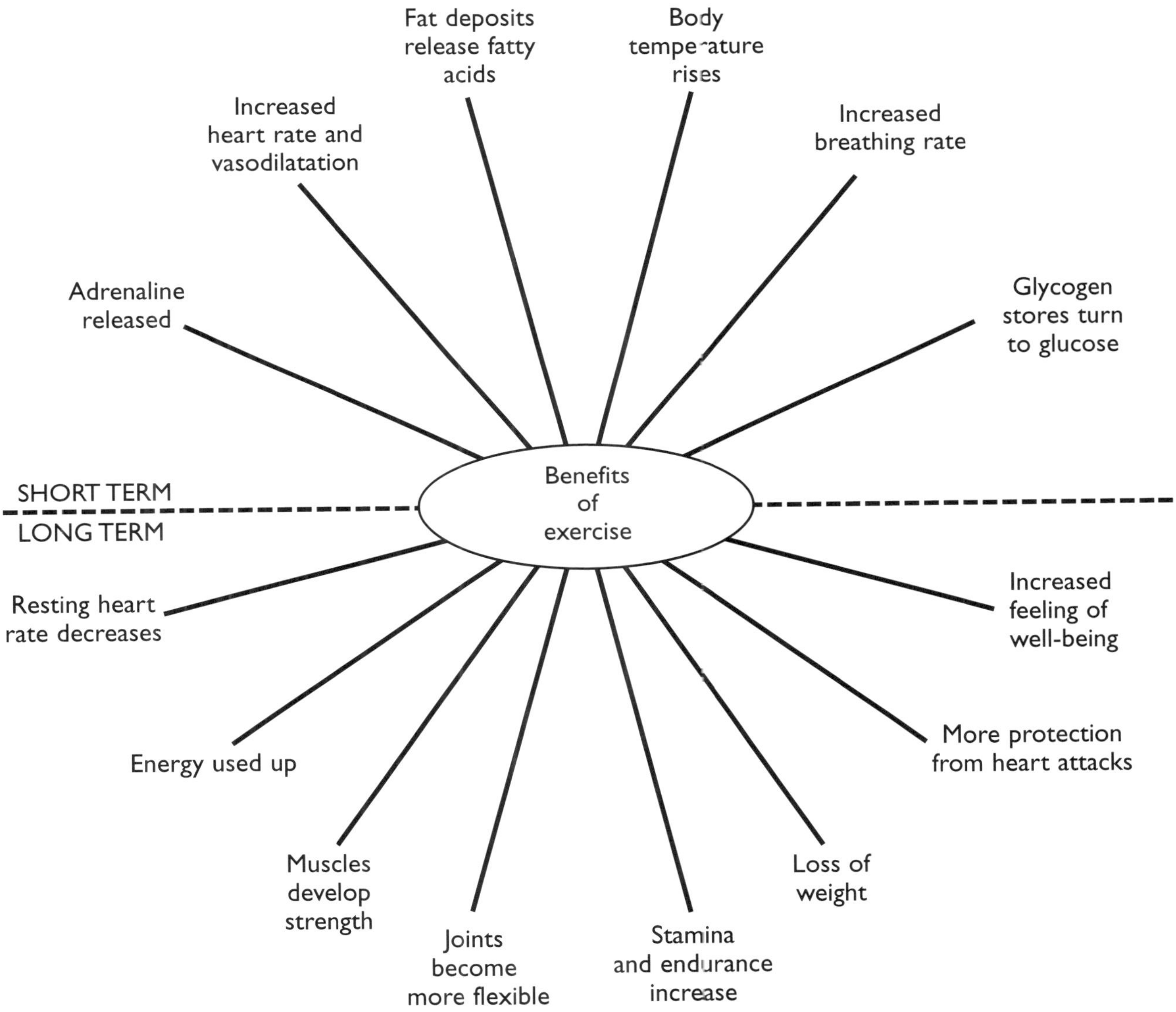
Fat deposits release fatty acids
Body temperature rises
Increased heart rate and vasodilatation
Increased breathing rate
Adrenaline released
Glycogen stores turn to glucose
Benefits of exercise
SHORT TERM
LONG TERM
Resting heart rate decreases
Increased feeling of well-being
Energy used up
More protection from heart attacks
Muscles develop strength
Loss of weight
Joints become more flexible
Stamina and endurance increase

THE BENEFITS OF EXERCISE TO HEALTH AND WELL-BEING

Activity	Cardiovascular health	Flexibility	Muscle strength and endurance
Aerobics	***	***	***
Badminton	**	***	**
Basketball	**	**	**
Cricket	*	**	**
Cycling	***	*	**
Hill walking	***	*	**
Hockey	**	*	**
Jogging	***	*	**
Netball	**	**	**
Rugby	**	**	**
Squash	**	**	**
Soccer	**	*	**
Swimming	***	***	**
Tennis	**	**	**
Volleyball	**	**	**
Weight training	*	***	***

*   Fair
**   Good
*** Very good

Note: Physical health benefits will vary with the level of effort put into the activity

ENERGY BALANCE

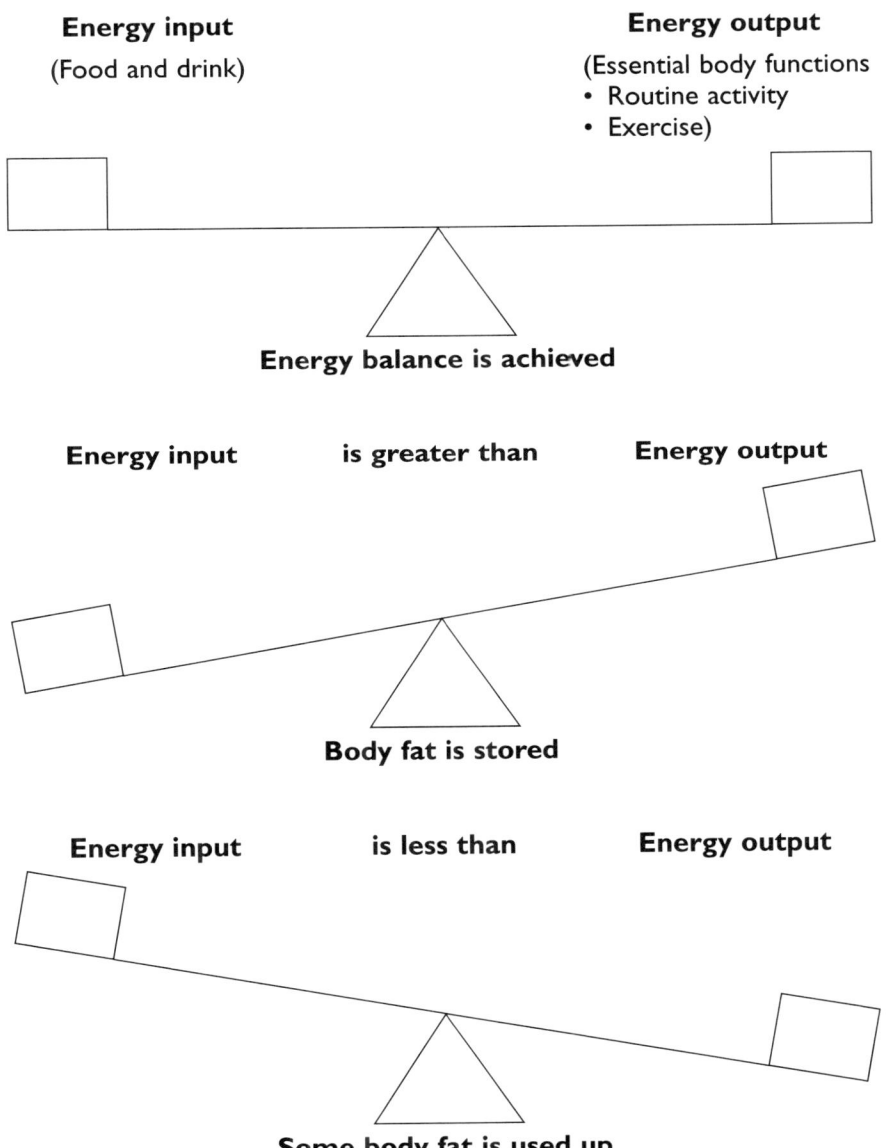

Energy input
(Food and drink)

Energy output
(Essential body functions
• Routine activity
• Exercise)

Energy balance is achieved

Energy input   **is greater than**   **Energy output**

Body fat is stored

Energy input   **is less than**   **Energy output**

Some body fat is used up

EFFECTS OF ALCOHOL ABUSE

Feeling good

Alcohol dependence

Loss of
self-control
– confusion

Short Term

Long Term

Cirrhosis
of liver

Social relationships
destroyed

Vulnerability to
accidents

Effects of
alcohol abuse

Lack of money

After initial
'high', depression

Slows reaction times
– brain areas affected

COMA

DEATH

Altered sexual
performance
– stimulates desire
but
weakens
performance

Weakened immune
system
– more infections

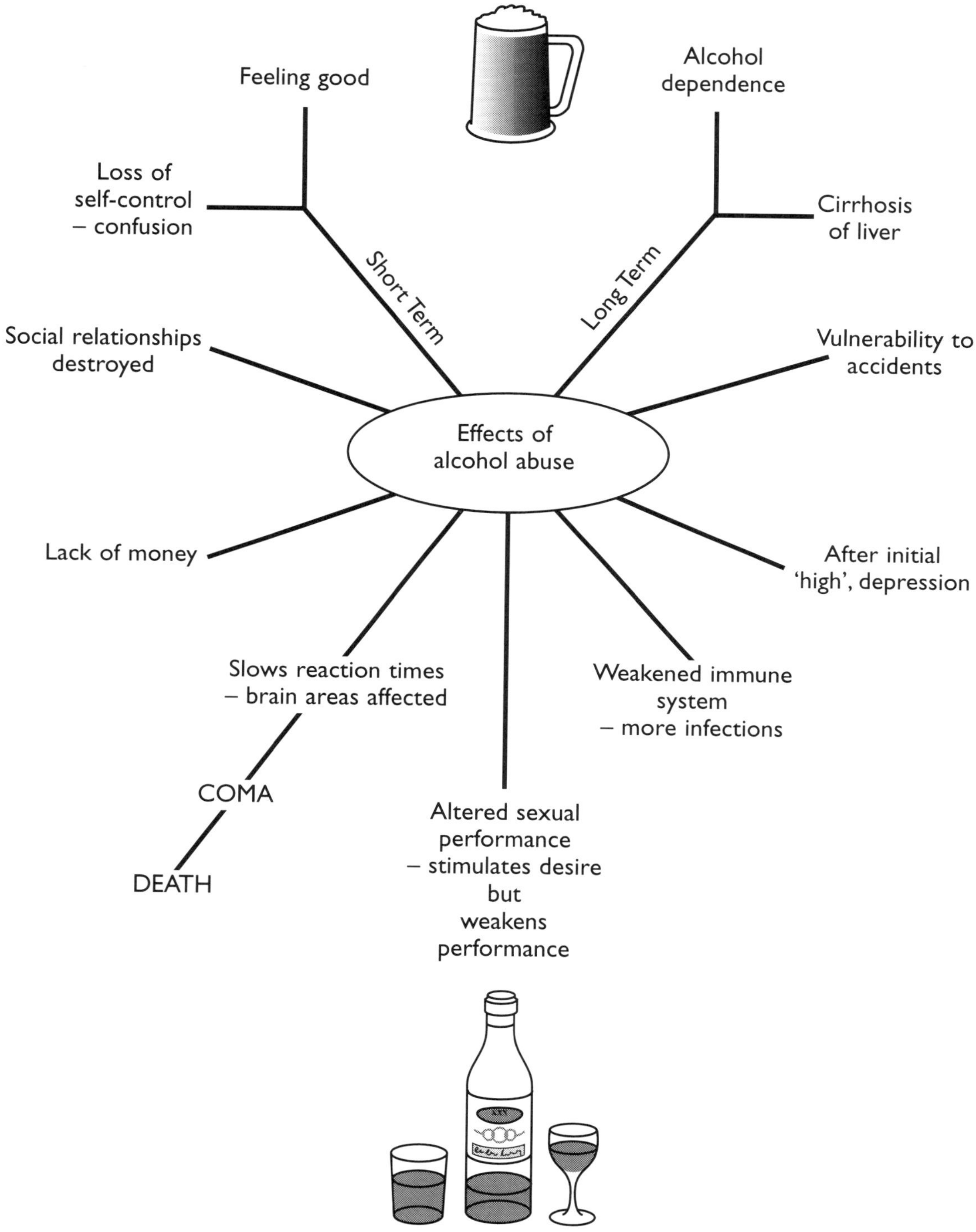

HARMFUL EFFECTS OF MISUSING DRUGS

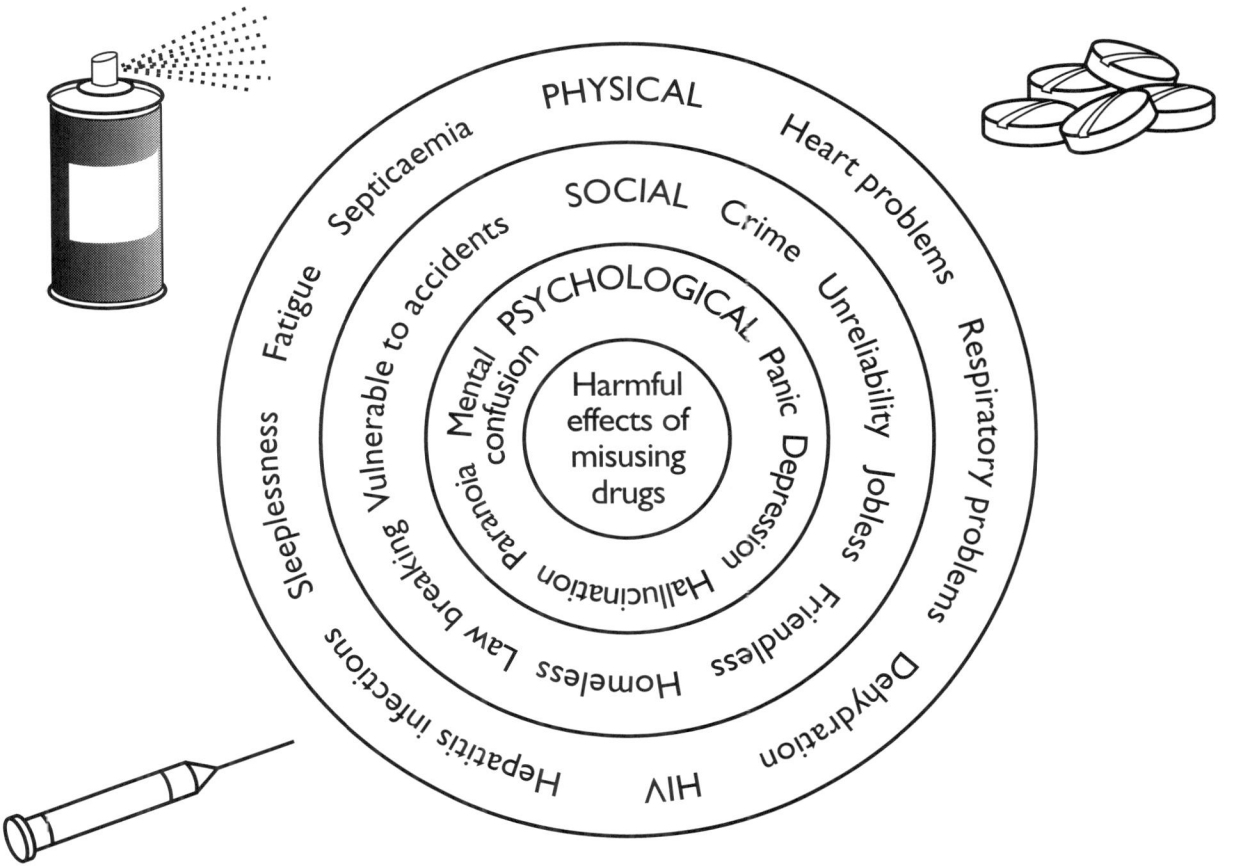

Harmful effects of misusing drugs

PHYSICAL: Septicaemia, Fatigue, Sleeplessness, Heart problems, Respiratory problems, Dehydration, HIV, Hepatitis infections

SOCIAL: Crime, Unreliability, Jobless, Friendless, Homeless, Law breaking, Vulnerable to accidents

PSYCHOLOGICAL: Mental confusion, Paranoia, Hallucination, Depression, Panic

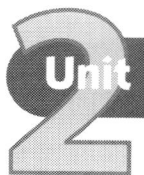

Student information sheet 9

HAZARDS OF SMOKING

Hazards of smoking

Tar causes cancers of the nose, throat, tongue, lungs, stomach and bladder

Nicotine causes:

- addiction
- increased blood clotting leading to thrombosis

Heart disease and poor circulation:

- increased blood pressure
- increased heart attacks
- narrowing of arteries

Irritant particles cause:

- bronchitis
- emphysema
- asthma
- smoker's cough

Exposure in pregnancy causes:

- smaller babies
- more stillbirths
- more miscarriages

Carbon monoxide causes:

- decreased oxygenation of cells and tissues
- poor growth (see pregnancy and childhood)
- extra work for the heart increases the risks of thrombosis

Exposure in childhood means that children:

- are prone to chest infections and asthma
- tend to be smaller and weaker
- do less well at school

ACCEPTABLE DAILY CONSUMPTION OF ALCOHOL

| I glass of wine = I unit | I half pint of beer/lager = I unit | I sherry = I unit | I measure of spirit = I unit |

Unit 2 Student information sheet 11

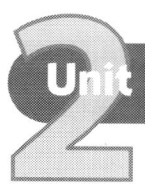

HEIGHT AND WEIGHT CHART

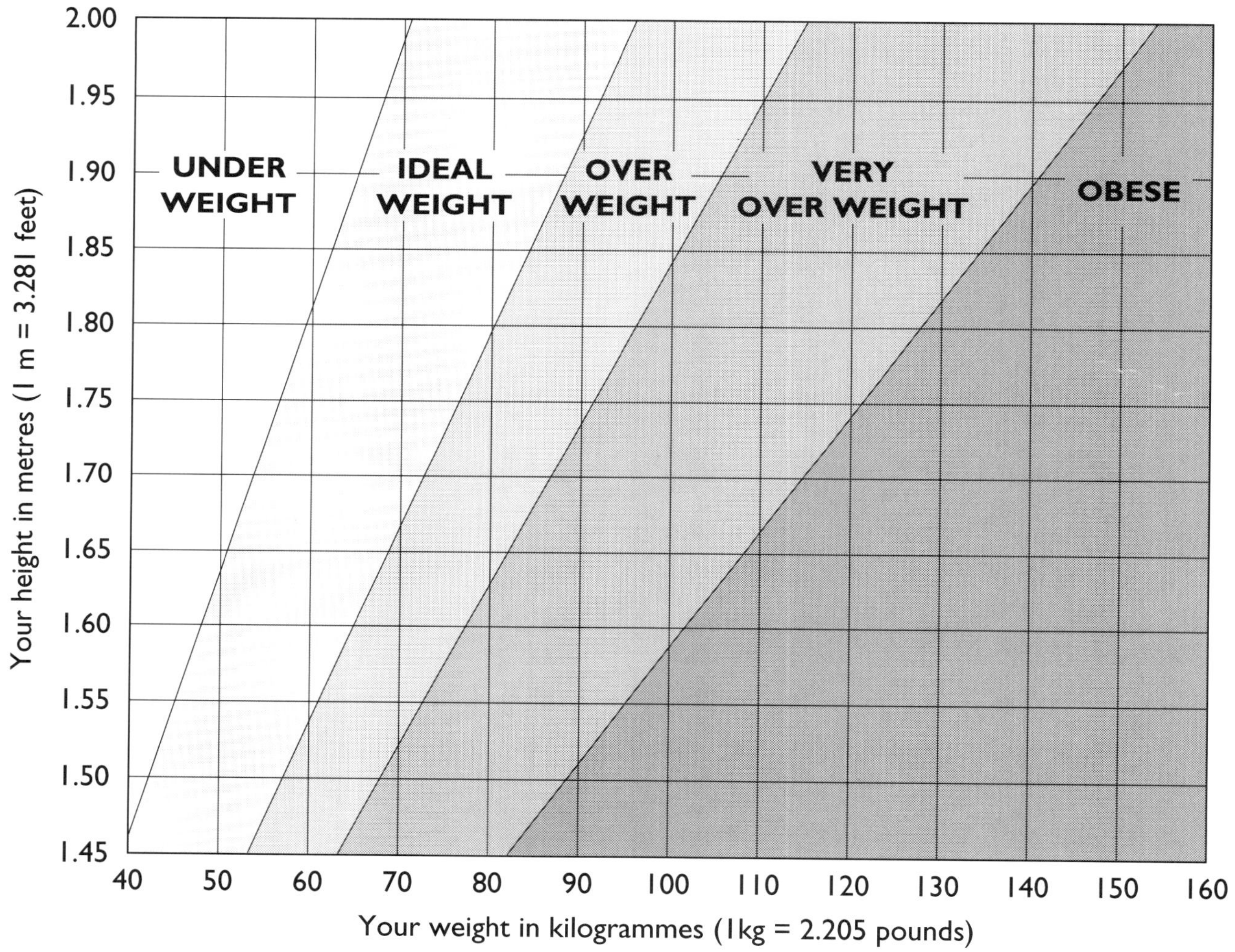

UNDER WEIGHT
IDEAL WEIGHT
OVER WEIGHT
VERY OVER WEIGHT
OBESE
2.00
1.95
1.90
1.85
1.80
1.75
1.70
1.65
1.60
1.55
1.50
1.45
Your height in metres (1 m = 3.281 feet)
40
50
60
70
80
90
100
110
120
130
140
150
160
Your weight in kilogrammes (1kg = 2.205 pounds)

WHAT DOES HEALTH AND WELL-BEING MEAN TO YOU?

1. The table below gives some statements about health. Individually, read them through, then tick the 'yes' or 'no' columns next to them.

2. Now decide which *five* statements are most important to you. Number your choices 1 to 5.

3. Working in small groups, compare the 'yes' statements and the priority numbers you have. What conclusions can you reach? Summarise your findings. Ask one of your group to report back to the whole group, summarising your findings.

Health statement	Yes, I agree	No, don't agree	Priority number 1 to 5
Not being ill			
Not being disabled			
Being the right weight for my height			
Taking regular exercise			
Eating plenty of fresh fruit and vegetables			
Forming good social relationships			
Not smoking			
Sleeping well at night			
Having enough money to do what you want			
Seeing my family doctor regularly			
Being even-tempered			
Taking very little alcohol			
Having no sex or practising safe sex			
Looking fit and sun-tanned			
Not feeling stressed			
Having a part-time job			
Having a hobby			
Not getting depressed			
Having somewhere nice to live			
Having your own personal space			
Having a pulse rate within expected norms			
Write your own statements below			

Read the following letters on a problem page.

Hi Michael and Emily.

I am writing to you because I do not know who else to turn to. I am very unhappy at school because I am a Muslim and other children keep calling me because of the terrorists who crashed planes into the World Trade Centre. They do not seem to understand that I am just as horrified as they are and that it is nothing to do with me or my family. What can I do to convince them?

Yours in desperation.

Ahmed

Dear Michael and Emily,

I am 13 years old and find myself in a very difficult situation. I have been invited to a party on Saturday and all my mates are going but I have found out that a boy I used to know at primary school is going and has got a supply of blow that he is going to take to the party. I do not want to go anywhere near drugs – I have been taught at school about the dangers of drug abuse – but do not want to miss out on a night out with my friends. Please tell me what to do?

Yours,

Thomas

Dear Michael and Emily,

I am 14 years old and go with my friends to a local shopping centre every Saturday. Boys seem to like me – last Saturday one pinched my bottom – but my parents have brought me up not to talk to strangers and not to let boys handle me in such a way. Last weekend a boy that I had spotted and fancied sent one of his friends over to ask me to go out with him. It was what I was hoping for but I am very shy and immediately said no. As soon as I had said it I regretted it. This is not the first time this has happened. What should I do next time this happens?

Best wishes,

Louise

1. Working with a partner try to identify which of the PIES (it might be more than one) each adolescent is having problems with in the situation described.

    Louise: _____

    Thomas: _____

    Ahmed: _____

2. Write a reply to each letter on the back of this worksheet or on a separate piece of paper.

Extension activity

▷ In a small group pick one of the letters above and role-play firstly the situation and secondly the person being given advice by Michael and Emily.

Unit 2 PIES for older people

1. Write down some of the health problems older people may have.

_____

_____

_____

2. Which of the needs of older people (see page 94 in GCSE Health and Social Care book) will be affected by a reduced income?

_____

_____

_____

_____

3. Which needs increase when they lose a much-loved partner?

_____

_____

_____

4. Are there any other PIES that are missing from the list? If so, what are they?

_____

_____

Extension activity

> **£18 MILLION ON WASTED MEALS IN NHS HOSPITALS EACH YEAR**
>
> One in three hospitals serve food cold and elderly patients rarely get the help they need to eat it which often results in the meal being taken away untouched. This means that up to 40 per cent of NHS patients are malnourished, a source revealed today.

1. Why do they think meals are often left untouched in NHS hospitals?

2. Make some brief notes here on the way older people are treated in hospital. You might need to refer to newspaper and magazine articles.

_____

_____

_____

_____

3. On the back of this worksheet write a letter to your local newspaper giving your opinions on the situation described. Put your point of view forcefully but politely i.e. be assertive.

Unit 2 PIES for disabled people

Case study

Shamma is 19 years old and has Down's Syndrome. She is very friendly and loves a good chat with anyone who is near her. She will engage strangers in conversation and is very affectionate. She gets a job at a local supermarket, packing bags at the checkouts for those customers who like some help with their packing.

1. Find out about Down's Syndrome by looking at the DSA website. A link can be found at www.heinemann.co.uk/hotlinks.

2. In a group work out Shamma's physical, intellectual, emotional and social needs.

    Physical: _____

    _____

    Intellectual: _____

    _____

    Emotional: _____

    _____

    Social: _____

    _____

3. Discuss how this job will meet Shamma's needs.

    Physical: _____

    _____

    Intellectual: _____

    _____

    Emotional: _____

    _____

    Social: _____

    _____

4. Are there any problems that Shamma might face?

    _____

    _____

    _____

5. How can the checkout assistant help with these problems?

    _____

    _____

Case study

Zeshan is six years old and is unable to walk due to a car accident two years ago. He now uses a wheelchair. He and his family are Muslims. Zeshan has to go into hospital to have an operation on his spine. His mother is going to stay at the hospital with him, until she knows he has come through the operation safely. He has several brothers and sisters and lots of other family live nearby. They live in a semi-detached house on a large estate on the edge of town. His father carries him up and down stairs but they are hoping to get help from social services to adapt the house or move to somewhere more suitable. His father was driving the car at the time of the accident and although it was not his fault he feels guilty and is very protective of Zeshan. His mother also fusses over him a lot. His brothers and sisters are sometimes a little jealous of the attention he gets but would not admit it and they are all very helpful and supportive of him.

1. Write down Zeshan's physical, intellectual, emotional and social needs.

Physical: _____

Intellectual: _____

Emotional: _____

Social: _____

2. Which of the needs you have identified are being met? Highlight or underline them.

3. How are they being met?

Physical: _____

Intellectual: _____

Emotional: _____

Social: _____

4. Which of Zeshan's needs are not being met? Highlight or underline them in a different colour. Add a key.

5. Make some suggestions as to how these needs can be met, taking into account his disability.

_____

_____

_____

6. What advice would you give to his parents?

_____

_____

7. What will the nurses and doctors have to take into account to make Zeshan's stay in hospital as acceptable as possible, given that Zeshan is a Muslim?

_____

_____

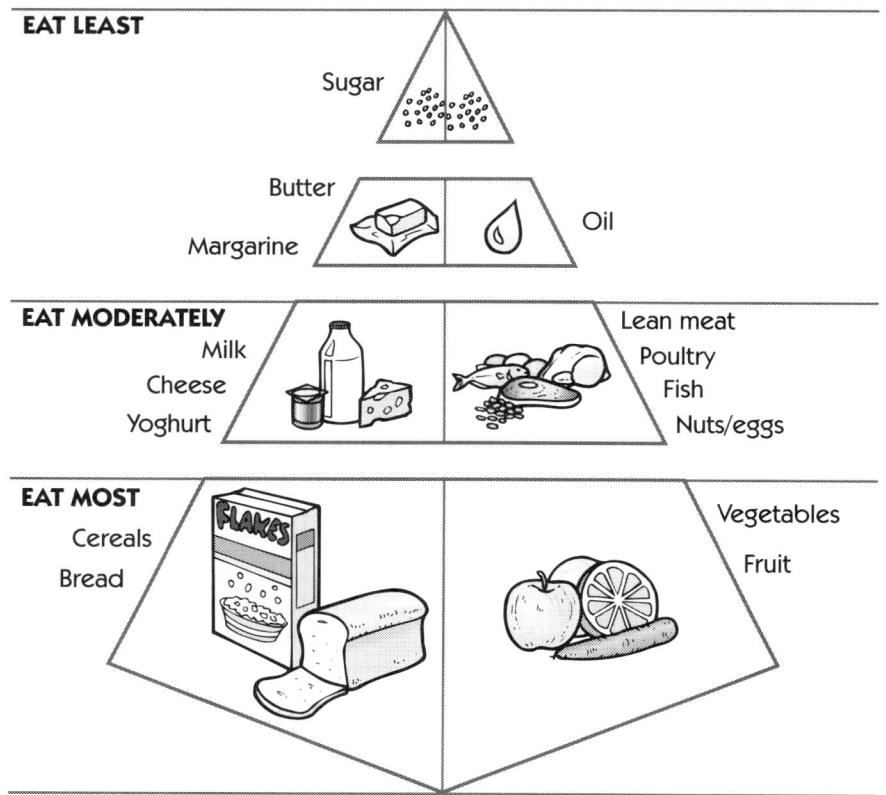

EAT LEAST
Sugar

Butter
Margarine
Oil

EAT MODERATELY
Milk
Cheese
Yoghurt
Lean meat
Poultry
Fish
Nuts/eggs

EAT MOST
Cereals
Bread
Vegetables
Fruit

Do the following activity in pairs.

1. Using a separate large sheet of paper for each, plan a day's meals (breakfast, lunch and tea) to give the following people a balanced, suitable diet:

   (a) a toddler who is two years old

   (b) an elderly woman who walks to the local shops and library for exercise each day

   (c) a teenager who dances two evenings a week and studies hard

   (d) a General Practitioner (doctor).

2. Below each course, in a different colour, explain what the nutrients are in each meal and how the combination you have decided on gives a balanced diet.

3. If you have time your teacher might ask you to stick your diet sheets on sugar paper to put on the wall so that you can compare your diets with those of others in your group.

Extension activity

▷ Pick one of the day's meals and state quantities for each item of food and drink. Explain why you have chosen those particular foods for that person.

Unit 2 Supportive relationships in adolescence

1. There are many relationships within families. Write down the physical, intellectual, emotional and social needs that each of the relationships below can provide for you as an adolescent and for the other family members concerned.

Parents

- Physical _____

  _____

- Intellectual _____

  _____

- Emotional _____

  _____

- Social _____

  _____

Siblings (brothers and sisters)

- Physical _____

  _____

- Intellectual _____

  _____

- Emotional _____

  _____

- Social _____

  _____

Grandparents

  _____

- Physical _____

  _____

- Intellectual _____

  _____

- Emotional _____

  _____

- Social _____

  _____

2. Discuss in groups of three or four how relationships are affected if you are:

- an only child

- the oldest child

- the youngest child in a large family

- the only girl in a family of boys.

3. Try to identify advantages and disadvantages for each of these which could affect your development. You don't need to write them down. Be aware when discussing these issues that someone in the group will be in one of these positions in their own family – remember to be sensitive to their feelings.

Extension activity

▷ How will relationships be affected if you are:

(a) a member of an extended family i.e. a family which includes grandparents, etc. living together or close to each other

_____

_____

_____

(b) a member of a nuclear family i.e. one where parents and children live together and other family members such as grandparents live some distance away

_____

_____

_____

Unit 2 Leisure activity

Work in a group of three or four. Your teacher will ask you to concentrate on a child, an adolescent, an adult, an elderly person or a person with a disability. Write which here.

Client group: _____

1. Write a list of at least 10 different leisure activities your person might pursue. Make them as varied as possible and do not name lots of different sports – the word sport would be just one activity.

    1. _____
    2. _____
    3. _____
    4. _____
    5. _____
    6. _____
    7. _____
    8. _____
    9. _____
    10. _____

2. On a piece of sugar paper or a flip chart write the words 'leisure activities' in a circle in the middle.

3. In each of the four corners write one of the following: Physical Needs, Intellectual Needs, Emotional Needs and Social Needs.

4. In each of the four sections, write the 10 activities your group has selected and by each one identify how it satisfies the person's needs in that section.

5. At the end of this activity one of you may be asked to report back to the rest of the class so make sure everyone contributes to the discussion.

Extension activity

1. Identify any change in circumstances that might cause problems for your person in pursuing these activities, for example, redundancy in the family or a car accident.

_____

_____

_____

_____

2. Pick one of the named changes. Identify alternatives, which will still allow your person to enjoy their leisure time and satisfy their physical, intellectual, emotional and social needs.

Change: _____

Alternatives: _____

_____

_____

_____

Walk round your school with a partner. Look for 10 different places where you think there is a hazard. Complete a risk assessment in the form of a table such as the one below:

Identify the hazard	Describe the hazard	Assess the risk on a scale of 1 to 5 (1 = low risk, 5 = high risk)	What is being done about it?	What could be done to improve matters?	Who should improve matters?	How soon should it be done?

Unit 2 Risk management in school (continued)

Extension activity

▷ Write a formal report of what you have discovered and present it to the school health and safety officer. Ask that teacher to come and talk to the class about what will be done, if anything, about the risks you have found, if they have time.

Find out what the law is on risk assessment in schools. The health and safety officer should be able to tell you this.

Unit 2 | Risk management in health and social care settings

1. List some of the health and social care services that you know quite well in your local area, for example, your own doctor's surgery, on the table below. Add the client group/s who use each one and in a group discuss what the possible risks might be with that particular client group in that particular setting.

Service	Client group/s	Risks

2. Divide the places you have thought of between you and see if you can arrange to go and visit a member of staff from the one you have been allocated to ask about potential risks and the techniques they use to manage those risks. Make some brief notes so you can report back to your group.

Extension activity

▷ Pool your results with those of the rest of your group to produce a report on how risk management techniques are used to protect individuals and promote personal safety in each of the settings you have visited between you. Word process the report. Present the information in an attractive and easily understood format.

Unit 2 Risks to health and well-being: choosing an assignment subject

At the end of this unit you will be asked to write a plan to help a real person improve their health. You need to start thinking about who you can base your plan on and this worksheet is designed to help you to identify this person. Ideally you need to pick someone who has both positive and negative factors. You have already learnt about the positive factors in Chapter 7 and you will learn about the risks to health in Chapter 8. The following table will help you to think about these positive and negative factors. You could photocopy this table several times and try applying it to yourself, family members and close friends to see who gives you a good balance of things to write about.

Name of person: _____

Age: _____

Positive factors	NOTES
Balanced diet	
Supportive relationships	
Adequate financial resources	
Stimulating work	
Stimulating education	
Stimulating leisure activity	
Health monitoring	
Safe, clean environment	
Good personal hygiene	
Time to relax	
Any other positive factor	

Negative factors	NOTES
Poor diet (underweight)/Unbalanced diet (overweight)	
Social isolation – no friends	
Poor/Unemployed	
Doesn't keep brain active	
Lack of exercise	
Disease e.g. cancer, diabetes, asthma	
Condition e.g. limp after an accident	
Drugs e.g. solvents, smoking, alcohol	
Inadequate housing/Pollution	
Lack of personal hygiene	
Stress	
Any other negative factor	

Unit 2 Genetically inherited diseases and conditions: cystic fibrosis

Worksheet 2.11
pages 124–126

Cystic fibrosis (CF) is the most common life-threatening inherited disease affecting babies and children in the UK. It clogs vital organs in the body such as the lungs with thick sticky mucus. Those with the disease have to have physiotherapy every day, which involves pounding on the back and chest, in order to remove this mucus. Every week three young people die from cystic fibrosis, often as a result of lung damage and infection leading to pneumonia.

1. How would cystic fibrosis affect a child's:

(i) physical needs?

_____

_____

(ii) intellectual needs?

_____

_____

(iii) emotional needs?

_____

_____

(iv) social needs?

_____

_____

2. How will a young child feel when a physiotherapist or a family member trained to clear the mucus has to treat them?

_____

_____

3. How will that physiotherapist or family member feel about having to treat the child like that every day?

_____

_____

4. The Cystic Fibrosis Trust is the only national charity in the UK which funds research to try to understand, treat and cure the diseases. Find out more about the condition on the Internet (see www.heinemann.co.uk/hotlinks).

Extension activity

▷ Do you think it is right that people have to raise money to allow this research to go on? Contact someone at the CF Trust or a similar body to find out what the Government is doing to support these causes.

Unit 2 Solvent abuse

Worksheet 2.12
pages 127–129

SCHOOL PUPILS RISKING THEIR LIVES FOR A KICK

Parents were horrified to find that evidence of solvent abuse has been found in the toilets at Highclass School in Goodway. A cleaner reported that he had found an assortment of empty aerosols and a milk bottle with a plastic tube attached to it. The head teacher has decided to go public and tell the parents what has happened so that they are aware there is a problem and can be on the lookout for any signs of solvent abuse in their children.

---

1. Do you think the head teacher should have just kept the problem within school or do you think he was right to inform the parents, even though it might mean bad publicity for the school? Explain why you think this.

Opinion.

_____

_____

Reason.

_____

_____

2. In order to help parents recognise the signs of solvent abuse and to raise pupils' awareness of the dangers, the head teacher runs a competition asking pupils to produce an information sheet. Imagine you are one of the pupils who enters the competition. Use the spider diagram on page 127 of the GCSE Health and Social Care book to help you design a suitable information sheet.

3. Suggest ways in which you could help a friend whom you discover has started to sniff glue to kick the habit, given that solvent abuse is often linked with some other more deeply hidden problem.

_____

_____

_____

_____

_____

Extension activity

▷ Find out what you should do if you find anyone who is unconscious due to the effects of solvent abuse. Find out what 'Sudden Sniffing Death' is. Produce a list of dos and don'ts and be prepared to share your findings with the rest of the class.

Unit 2 Smoking

Discuss the following in a small group.

1. The government discourages smoking by making it illegal to sell cigarettes to those under 16 years of age, by displaying health warnings and by limiting cigarette advertising. Do you think this is enough?

    _____

    _____

    _____

    _____

    _____

2. What would you do to persuade young people not to smoke if you were in a position to do so?

    _____

    _____

    _____

    _____

3. In your group, write a television advert to discourage young people from smoking. Include music or anything else you think will get the message across. Practise acting out your advertisement, ready to show the rest of the group.

4. Design a leaflet to discourage young people from smoking. Word-process it if possible. Think carefully about what you should include and don't make it too cluttered. Make sure you include some proven facts about the effects of smoking.

Extension activity

▷ Arrange a time to have a video camera to use. Record your advert. Watch it afterwards and discuss

   •   what worked well
   •   what didn't work well
   •   what you could do to improve it.

   Make the improvements and re-record it. Show the advert to the rest of the group and ask for their opinion on it afterwards.

Look at the tables showing HIV infected individuals and AIDS cases by exposure category.

United Kingdom data: HIV infected individuals by exposure category

How HIV infection was probably acquired	HIV			
	Males	**Females**	**Total**	**%**
Sex between men	27419		27419	55
Sex between men and woman	6084	8101	14185	
Injecting drug user	2623	1190	3813	8
Blood/tissue transfer or blood factor	1498	193	1691	3
Mother to infant	416	402	818	2
Other/undetermined	1231	5`3	1744	4
Total	**39271**	**10399**	**49670**	**100%**
Percentage total	**79%**	**21%**	**100%**	

AIDS cases by exposure category

How HIV infection was probably acquired	AIDS			
	Males	**Females**	**Total**	**%**
Sex between men	12001		12001	65
Sex between men and woman	1995	1913	3908	
Injecting drug user	817	328	1145	86
Blood/tissue transfer or blood factor	737	1)3	840	5
Other/undetermined	407	329	646	3
Total	**15957**	**25B3**	**18540**	**100%**
Percentage total	**86%**	**214%**	**100%**	

(Source: Public Health Laboratory Service AIDS Centre)

1. Find the percentage of HIV infected persons who were injecting drug users. _____

2. Find the percentage of AIDS cases in people who were injecting drug users. _____

3. Draw two bar charts, one to show how HIV infection was probably acquired for males and one for females, to the same scale.

4. What do you notice when you compare the two bar charts?

_____

_____

Extension activity

1. Calculate the percentage of people with HIV infected by the heterosexual route.

   _____

   _____

2. Repeat this for those with AIDS infected by the heterosexual route.

   _____

   _____

3. What do you think some of the other/undetermined ways of acquiring HIV infection might be?

   _____

   _____

4. Why do you think the heading of the first column says 'probably'?

   _____

   _____

Unit 2

The effects of inadequate housing on a young child

Complete the table below to show how each factor might affect a young child's health. The first one has been done for you.

Factors affecting health and well-being	Physically	Intellectually	Emotionally	Socially
No garden	Less chance of exercise and fresh air	Less fresh air so mind less alert	Cooped up when no-one can take her/him out	Less chance to play out and make new friends
Damp				
Noise				
Overcrowding				
Living in city centre				
Living in high rise flat				
Cleanliness				
Unpleasant smells from local factory				
Littered stairwells and pavements				
Poor heating				

Extension activity

▷ Copy out the table but this time complete it for the effects on a member of a different client group, for example, an elderly or disabled person.

Unit 2 Height and weight charts

1. Read the case studies below and use a height/weight chart to see which weight range each person falls into.

2. Identify what each person could do to improve her or his health.

3. Write down what you would say to each person to persuade them to follow a proper plan to produce these improvements.

Case study

Lisa has a part-time job in a fast food outlet that she goes to straight after college. As she never has time for a meal first, she is extremely hungry by the time she gets to her comfort break around nine o'clock. Most nights she has a burger and chips at that time. Lisa is 1.480 m and weighs 53.5 kg. She would be classed as an average frame size. She always seems to be tired as she frequently doesn't get home until 1 a.m. and is on her feet most of the night. If she refuses hours, the threat of sacking is raised.

Case study

Tony lives at home and is a keen footballer in his spare time. He doesn't have a part-time job because his parents are able to support him financially. He misses a lot of classes with excuses about playing football matches and is often late in the mornings. Surprisingly, Tony smokes at least 20 cigarettes every day and drinks about 9 pints of beer every night. Tony is 1.730 m tall and weighs 60.7 kg; his frame is small for his height.

Case study

Vik is of small stature and weighs only 55.7 kg for a height of 1.625 m. His cultural background is Indonesian but he is second generation British. Vik has to spend most of his free time helping in his parents' shop and has no time to socialise with his peers. He has no friends as they have long since stopped asking him to go out with them. He is very reserved in class and often feels depressed that he has no friends. His parents prefer him to mix with 'his own kind' and cannot see any problem that hard work won't cure.

Case study

Tasha is two years older than her peers. She has had some time off school due to personal difficulties and was taken into care. She is now trying to catch up on her education as she would like to be a social worker herself. Tasha is a tall, willowy young woman with a slender frame; she is 1.780 m tall and 55.3 kg in weight. She is extremely quiet and knows that she needs to work on her communication skills to succeed in her ambitions.

Case study

Tessa is a large-framed girl who loves to play netball and swim. She is tall and fairly heavy. Tessa seems to get on well with all her peers and seems to be both popular and even-tempered. Recently, she started to take some drugs from her new boyfriend. It was just a laugh at first but it seems to be becoming a daily habit now. Tessa knows she should stop, but is afraid that her boyfriend will finish with her if she does. He takes drugs himself, but is good fun to be with. Tessa is 1.650 m tall and 65.5 kg in weight.

Notes

_____

_____

_____

_____

_____

_____

_____

_____

_____

_____

_____

_____

_____

_____

_____

_____

_____

_____

_____

_____

_____

Unit 2 Blood pressure

Facts

- A piece of scientific research has shown that a new drug that lowers blood pressure could reduce the number of deaths by 40 per cent compared with other blood pressure drugs.

- The drug also reduces the risk of diabetes developing in high-risk patients by 25 per cent.

- Doctors now want the drug to be available to everyone at risk of developing diabetes.

- At present there are at least 1.4 million people in Britain affected by a particular type of diabetes and it is predicted that by 2010 the number of cases will rise to three million.

- The new drug costs at least three times as much as other blood pressure drugs to prescribe.

- People with diabetes are at increased risk of stroke and heart disease.

- One in five people with high blood pressure are twice as likely to develop diabetes as other people.

1. Do you think this drug should be made readily available despite the cost? Yes/No

2. Why do you think this?

_____

_____

_____

3. Why do you think that doctors are so keen to stop diabetes developing?

_____

_____

_____

4. What are the other risks of having high blood pressure?

_____

_____

_____

5. High blood pressure can cause small haemorrhages in the retina. Why is it therefore important to have a regular eye test?

_____

_____

Extension activity

▷ Low blood pressure can sometimes be the result of Parkinson's disease. This is a condition that occurs when cells in the part of the brain controlling movement die. There is no cure as yet because it is not known why these cells die, but a new treatment is being cautiously welcomed. It repairs these cells and relieves the symptoms, thereby improving the patient's quality of life. Doctors say there is a need for more trials yet, in case there are serious side effects.

Discuss in a group whether you think that such a treatment should be available to people with Parkinson's disease if they want it, even though trials are still taking place.

OBESE TEENAGERS AT RISK OF DIABETES

Doctors have warned today that obese teenagers are at risk of developing adult diabetes, normally seen in adults aged over 40. The first cases in the UK, four teenagers aged 13 to 15, have recently been diagnosed. All four had Body Mass Indexes of over 32, in one case 40.6. A normal BMI is between 20 and 25 and over 30 is obese. Recent research showed that the number of overweight children had almost doubled in the last 10 years and the number of obese children had increased by 50 per cent.

Read the newspaper article above and answer the following questions:

1. Why do you think the number of overweight and obese children has increased so much in recent years?

_____

_____

_____

2. Do you think that this increase will continue? Why?

_____

_____

_____

3. What does Body Mass Index mean?

_____

_____

_____

4. The calculation of Body Mass Index involves doing some maths. Do you think it is a good indicator for a teenager to use? Why do you think this?

_____

_____

_____

5. Suggest three different ways that teenagers can control their weight.

_____

_____

_____

6. What other health risks are associated with obesity?

_____

_____

Extension activity

▷ Find out why obesity can lead to Type-2 diabetes. Prepare a short talk on how it can be controlled.

Alicia and Emma measured their pulse rates when they were sitting relaxing. They then exercised for 4 minutes and recorded their pulse rates every minute from the time they started exercising until their pulse rates were back to normal, a period of about 20 minutes. The results are shown in the table below.

Name of girl	Alicia	Emma
Time in minutes	**Pulse rate in pulse per minute**	**Pulse rate in pulse per minute**
0	80	60
1	100	80
2	120	100
3	140	120
4	160	140
5	150	130
6	140	120
7	130	110
8	120	100
9	110	90
10	107	85
11	104	80
12	101	75
13	98	70
14	96	65
15	93	61
16	90	60
17	88	61
18	86	60
19	84	61
20	82	60

1. Plot a graph in the space below with time in minutes on the x-axis (the bottom) and pulse rate in pulse per minute on the y-axis (up the side), with lines for both girls plotted on the same set of axes. Label each line so that you can see which applies to which girl.

2. Look at the graph and decide which girl is fittest. _____

3. Why do you think this?   (i) _____

                             (ii) _____

                             (iii) _____

Extension activity

▷ If you exercise regularly, how will it affect your:

- muscles? _____

_____

- heart? _____

_____

- breathing? _____

_____

Complete the following table by suggesting suitable health materials for use in a variety of different situations. In each case, give reasons for your choice of materials. You may choose to use more than one type of health promotion material. Re-read Chapter 10 of the textbook to remind yourself of the variety of health promotion materials that are available.

Client group	Choice of health promotion materials	Reasons for your choice
Women at an ante-natal clinic, most of whom are having their first baby		
Members of a youth club where it is known that illegal drugs are used		
Elderly residents in sheltered housing who need to be persuaded of the benefits of exercise		
Middle aged business people, many of whom need to lose weight		
A group of women from an ethnic minority who need to know about dental care		
A young child and her parents who need to know about the child's future immunisation		
Teenage girls who are known to 'binge drink' at the weekends		
Pregnant women who need to be informed of the effects of alcohol and smoking on their unborn babies		
Contraceptive advice to be given to young teenagers at school		

Unit 2 Health promotion

Choose two or three health promotion leaflets from the selection provided by your teacher. Make sure they cover different subjects e.g. do not choose three anti-smoking leaflets.

You are to write a report on the usefulness of the leaflets that you have chosen, comparing the leaflets with each other.

Before you start this piece of work, select your leaflets carefully. There will be more to say if you choose leaflets that differ greatly from each other. Try and choose one with many pictures and one with few. Or you could choose a leaflet with a lot of information in small print to compare with a leaflet that has only a little information in larger print.

When writing your report, consider the following points:

- Decide whom the information is aimed at, adults, teenagers etc.

- How easy is the information to understand?

- How is the leaflet set out – does the print vary, do they use bullet points, how big is the print?

- What type of illustrations are used, photographs and/or diagrams/drawings?

- Are the illustrations helpful to your understanding of the information, do they make the leaflet more attractive?

- Who has produced the leaflet?

- Is there a possibility of finding out more information about the subject of the leaflet i.e. does it include helpful addresses or websites?

- Make comments about the overall attractiveness of the leaflet – does it catch your attention and if so, how does it do that?

Extension activity

▷ Now use a suitable computer program to produce your own health promotion material such as a leaflet or handout sheet. Make sure you make it clear who your target audience is and use language to suit it. Also, ensure that your facts are correct. Include an image or graph or bar chart to provide more information and to add interest to your work.

Below are some details about Martin. As you can see, he needs some assistance to devise a health plan to improve his health.

Read the description of his health as it is at present and then complete the table to show how he could change his health behaviour over a reasonable length of time. When devising the plan, try to think of suitable alternatives that can be used to help him achieve his goals e.g. the use of Nicorette gum as a smoking substitute.

In the first column, list the risks to Martin's health if he does not change his behaviour. In the second column, list the stages he will need to go through to achieve successfully a change in his behaviour. In the third column, give a realistic time to enable him to achieve each stage.

Key facts about Martin

- Martin is 23 years old
- He is in good physical health
- He is not overweight
- He is a member of the pub football team
- He has smoked since he was fifteen. He smokes about 30 cigarettes a day
- He tends to 'binge' drink, particularly at the weekends
- He has a good social life but does not have a regular girlfriend

Stopping smoking

Risks to health from smoking	Stages in giving up	Timescale to achieve each stage

Cutting down on his alcohol intake

Risks to health from excess drinking	Stages in cutting down	Timescale to achieve each stage

Unit 3 Understanding personal development and relationships

Overview

This unit focuses on the personal development and relationships of the individual. It is important to stress at all times the effect that each factor studied has on the person's development in terms of PIES.

Unit 3 is externally assessed through a written test. When teaching the unit, the following ideas should be considered, to ensure accurate coverage of the concepts in each chapter.

Chapter 11 – Human growth and development

All aspects of the PIES need to be taught, with reference to all age groups. This can be difficult as there is, for example, plenty of information available on physical development of babies, but much less information on emotional development of adults. Students should be helped to understand the differences between social and emotional development. The elderly should not be automatically stereotyped as being infirm and in need of care. To counteract this, the positive aspects of retirement should be stressed or positive role models used to break down traditional ideas about the elderly.

Teaching tip

Students tend to have very fixed, stereotypical ideas about elderly people that are often rather derogatory. Teachers could try to overcome these ideas by collecting pictures of older people that show them doing various activities associated with younger people, such as running, carrying out heavy physical work or dealing with small children. Alternatively, pictures of attractive older people (both well known and unknown) could be used to try and break down the students' misconceptions about older people.

Activity

Ask the students to collect pictures of people from a range of age groups in preparation for the theory work to be covered in Unit 3. The pictures could be used to complete activities from the textbook or to add illustrations to their notes.

Chapter 12 – Factors that affect growth and development

Students should be able to differentiate between factors and identify them as physical, social and emotional, economic and environmental. They should be able to understand how numbers of factors interrelate to affect the personal development of the individual.

Teaching tip

This is a more difficult chapter as the work is very theoretical and requires students to analyse concepts that they will not have recognised before. As an introduction, the following ideas could be considered.

Students could be asked to consider the childhood and family background of well-known, successful people and then consider what effect the celebrity's background may have had on their eventual success. For example, the comedian Billy Connolly came from a very poor home and had a drunken father who sexually abused him. The DJ Chris Evans came from a single parent family who lived in a council flat in Warrington. (You could use any relevant examples that you and your students are likely to know of.) By looking at the person's background and their life now, students are being introduced to the link between different factors and a person's growth and development.

Alternatively, newspaper articles on the background of notorious criminals (or suspects) could be studied to illustrate how sociologists and psychologists carefully investigate the background of a person to try to find an explanation for their deviant behaviour. Again, students can be encouraged think about a link between different factors and the growth and development of the individual.

Chapter 13 – Effect of relationships on personal development

Students should be able to distinguish between different types of relationships and their relative influence on personal development. They should be aware of the effects of positive and negative relationships on development.

Activity

Ask the students to list the people they come into contact with every day. (Do not ask them to name every fellow student that they speak to or the list will go on forever!) They should think in terms of different individuals and groups of people e.g. friends, each parent, each sibling, other family members, neighbours, teachers, etc. They should then list them in order of importance to them and compare the lists within the group to look for similarities and differences. Explain to the students that chapter 13 looks at how different groups of people affect the development of the individual, as they have just been doing.

Chapter 14 – Self-concept

Initially, students need an understanding of what the self-concept is. This can be explained as 'outward looking' i.e. how you see yourself as a person and 'inward looking' i.e. what you think about yourself. Students then have to have an understanding of the various factors that affect the self-concept and how these factors can affect the person in a positive or negative way.

Activity

Ask each student to write a list of points that describe him or herself. Do not discuss the list now. At the end of the chapter (or at a point that you consider appropriate), discuss the students' lists. Hopefully the students should now be able to give a fuller, more detailed view of their self-concept, in comparison with their first attempt.

Chapter 15 – The effects of life events on personal development

Life events can be divided into expected and unexpected events. All will have an effect on the personal development of the individual. Different people will need different types of support depending on their age, family structure and the life event they are facing.

Activity

Ask students to list significant life events that they or their close family have experienced. They should then take one life event and list the people that helped them at that time. A typical event could be starting school, the birth of a sibling or the death of a grandparent. With help, the students could then divide the list into professional help and the help of family and friends. Ask volunteers to read out their lists. In a group, ask the students for suggestions of other people who could have helped in the situation that has been described.

Resources

Useful organisations

British Heart Foundation
14, Fitzhardinge Street
London
WH1 4DH

Carers National Association
20-25 Glasshouse Yard
London
EC1A 4JS

Cruse Bereavement Care
Cruse House
126 Sheen Road
Richmond
TW9 1UR

Department of Health
Richmond House
79 Whitehall
London
SW1A 2NS

Housing Corporation Headquarters
Maple House
149 Tottenham Court Road
London
W1T 7BN

Relate
Herbert Gray College
Little Church Street
Rugby
CV21 3AP

The Samaritans
The Upper Mill
Kingston Road
Ewell
Surrey
KT17 2AF

Social Care Association
Thornton House
Hook Road
Surbiton
Surrey
KT6 5AN

Useful websites

Links to useful websites can be found at www.heinemann.co.uk/hotlinks.

ADOLESCENT PHYSICAL CHANGES

Major female physical changes are:

- gains weight
- grows body hair
- periods start
- breasts develop
- shape changes
- skin and hair change
- becomes taller.

Major male physical changes are:

- gains weight
- grows body hair
- penis and testicles develop
- voice 'breaks'
- shoulders broaden
- skin and hair change
- shape changes
- becomes taller.

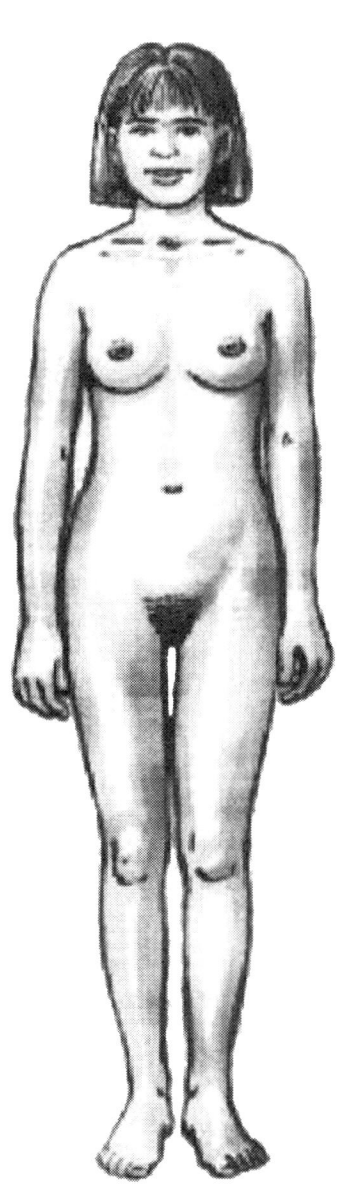

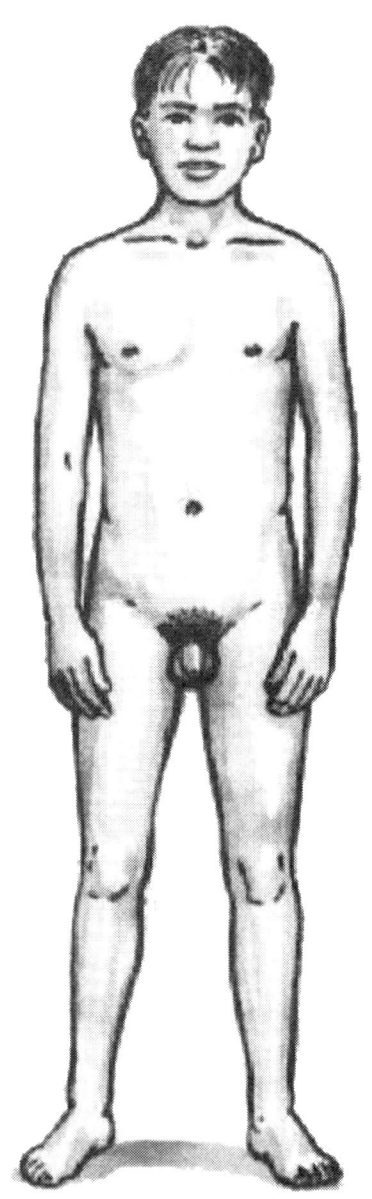

Student information sheet 2

PHYSICAL, INTELLECTUAL, EMOTIONAL AND SOCIAL DEVELOPMENT OF INFANTS (0–4)

Note – Gross and fine motor skills are being acquired at the same time.

Age of child	Physical development	Intellectual development	Emotional development	Social development
New born	Primitive reflexes only. Can see, smell, taste, hear, feel pain.	Startled by loud, sudden noises.	Cries when hungry or wet.	Sleeps for much of the day and night, aware of surroundings and people when awake.
One month	Stares at carer's face when feeding. Eyes follow moving object. Shuts eyes in bright light.	Responds to soothing voice if upset.	Stops crying when picked up.	Beginning to smile. Sleeps between feeds.
Three months	Makes a wider variety of sounds. Watches movement of own hands.	Recognises main carer's voice before being touched. Turns to sounds that he recognises e.g. bath times.	Coos and smiles a lot.	Enjoys bath and caring routines e.g. feeding, cuddling.
Six months	If held securely, can bear his own weight.	Responds to his own name and different tones in carer's voice. Makes a wide variety of sounds.	Screams when annoyed.	Takes everything into his mouth. Tries to help (patting bottle) when being fed.
Nine months	Noises he makes begin to sound like words. Very aware of his surroundings.	Looks for fallen toy in the right direction. Understands 'no' and 'bye bye'. Makes sounds, listens and then makes sounds again.	A strong bond should now be established between the child and his carer – the attachment relationship.	Holds own bottle or cup to try and feed. Plays 'peek-a-boo'.
One year old	Drinks from a cup with help. Watches things that are happening intently.	Imitates adults enthusiastically. Understands simple instructions. Has three or more words. Points out objects.	Likes to be within sight of adults he knows, can show affection by hugs etc.	Waves 'bye bye when asked. Doesn't put objects in his mouth as much as before.
Eighteen months	Begins to use pencils and can 'draw' on paper. Can walk downstairs. Can roll and throw a ball.	Has a vocabulary of about fifteen words. Interested in his image in the mirror.	Can be 'clingy' to main carer because he doesn't like separation from carer.	Feeds himself. Cries when left with people he doesn't know.
Two/three years old	Can ride on a sit-on toy.	Uses two word sentences e.g. 'Mummy gone'. Has a vocabulary of 200 words. As language improves, begins to ask questions. Beginning to be dry and free of nappies.	Does opposite of what he is told. Throws tantrums when he doesn't get his own way – 'the terrible twos'. Does not like separation from parents. Expresses violent emotions.	Copies actions of parents. Plays alongside other children – parallel play. Tends to be possessive with toys, he is not yet able to share.
Three/four years old	Can draw a face. Can put on and take off his own coat. Able to stand on one leg.	Talks well, asks questions and understands answers.	Happy to be left for a short time with people he doesn't know. Affectionate with parents.	Beginning to play with other children – co-operative play. May create imaginary friend.

PHYSICAL, INTELLECTUAL, EMOTIONAL AND SOCIAL DEVELOPMENT OF YOUNG CHILDREN (4–10)

Age of child	Physical development	Intellectual development	Emotional development	Social development
Four/five years old	Dresses herself, drawings becoming more complicated.	Talks clearly, uses basic grammar in speech.	Feels proud of her achievements, helps to develop high self-esteem.	Plays with other children, becoming competitive. Games are linked to the child's sex.
Six/seven years old	Adult teeth start to come through. Improved balance makes climbing, hopping easier. Fine motor skills greatly developed e.g. can tie shoelaces. Writing improving steadily.	Child's attention span is getting longer. Reading, writing and language steadily improving. Has an understanding of what numbers represent. Understands right and wrong.	Looks for more personal responsibility e.g. looking after her possessions. Can be shy with strangers.	Still plays in mixed sex groups. Enjoys teasing others.
Eight/nine years old	Body movements become smoother. Sports skills improve. Handwriting instead of printing of letters.	Can tell the time. Knows the date and has an understanding of time in the future. Can multiply and divide. Can do everyday sums e.g. working out change in a shop.	Needs the approval of others. Tends to hero worship people. Gaining independence from parents/carers, likes to show that she is an individual.	Tends to play in same sex groups. Joins clubs and teams.
Ten+ years old	Good gross and fine motor control. Writes for long periods with good speed.	Interested in world affairs. Continued improvement in Maths and English.	Seeks more independence. Understands honesty and fairness. More understanding of the relationships of others.	Attitudes and opinions of the peer group become increasingly important. Same sex friendships.

THE HOLMES–RAHE SCALE

Life event	Value
Death of partner	100
Divorce	73
Marital separation	65
Going to prison	63
Death of a close family member	63
Personal injury or illness	53
Marriage	50
Being dismissed at work	47
Marital reconciliation	45
Retirement	45
Change in health of family member	44
Pregnancy	40
Sexual difficulties	39
Gaining a new family member	39
Business or work adjustment	39
Business or work adjustment	39
Change in financial state	38
Death of a close friend	37
Change to different line of work	36
Change in number of arguments with partner	35
Mortgage larger than one year's net salary	31
Foreclosure of mortgage or loan	30
Change in responsibilities at work	29
Son or daughter leaving home	29
Trouble with in-laws	29
Outstanding personal achievement	28
Partner begins or stops work	26
Begin or end school	26
Change in living conditions	25
Revision of personal habits	24
Trouble with boss	23
Change in work hours or conditions	20
Change in residence	20
Change in schools	20
Change in recreation	19
Change in religious activities	19
Change in social activities	18
Mortgage or loan less than one year's net salary	17
Change in sleeping habits	16
Change in number of family get-togethers	15
Change in eating habits	15
Holiday	13
Major festival, e.g. Christmas	12
Minor violations of the law	11

Reproduced with permission from Elsevier Science Inc.

GROWTH PROFILES FROM BIRTH TO ADOLESCENCE

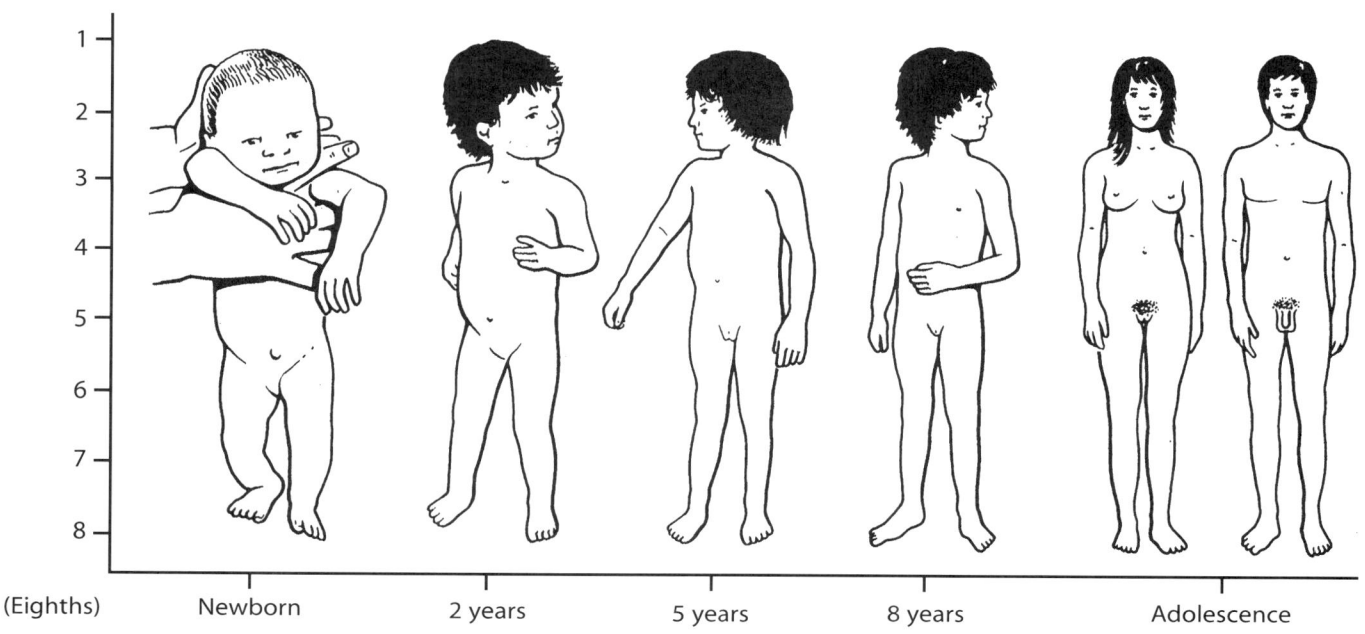

(Eighths)   Newborn   2 years   5 years   8 years   Adolescence

Unit 3 The nature versus nurture debate

Case study

Ben and Jonathon are twin brothers. They were only three months old when their parents were killed in a car crash. As they had no other family members to look after them, they were put up for adoption. Two different families adopted them and as they were so young they were not told about the fact that each had a twin brother for many years.

A couple that lived in London adopted Ben. Ben's father was very ambitious and had a job in a London bank. He worked very long hours and earned a good salary. His mother returned to work when Ben was four. She was a solicitor for a large firm in the City of London. Ben was encouraged to work hard at school. He was taken on expensive holidays and by the time he was sixteen, he had visited many different places around the world. After he finished school, he went to University. He then got a job in a City firm, selling stocks and shares. He soon earned a good salary and was able to buy his own flat in the centre of London. He still enjoyed his holidays and tried to combine foreign travel with sporting activities like sailing or skiing.

A couple from the Midlands adopted Jonathon. His father was a teacher. His mother did not work until Jonathon was seven, when she returned to work as a nurse at the local hospital. His parents were keen churchgoers and Jonathon was confirmed when he was ten years old. Every year, his parents became involved in fundraising for a local charity. Jonathon was encouraged to help them. He worked hard at school and after going to University, decided that he wanted to be a social worker, working with children. Around this time, his parents told him that he had a twin brother.

Jonathon enjoyed his work as a social worker. He remained a member of the Church and eventually married a girl who was also a churchgoer. Through his job as a social worker, he knew how to trace his twin. He eventually tracked down his brother and shortly after their thirtieth birthday, they met.

Ben and Jonathon meet for the first time in thirty years

Case study (continued)

It was a strange experience for both of them. They looked alike although Ben's hair was a lot shorter than Jonathon's. They discovered that they both supported the same football team and enjoyed reading historical novels. They had both had measles and each had a birthmark on their left hand. The meeting passed very quickly and they made arrangements to contact each other again. It had been a very happy, if unusual afternoon.

Read the case study carefully. List the characteristics that the men seemed to have acquired through nature. Then list the ones that seem to have been acquired through nurture.

	Nature	Nurture
Ben		
Jonathon		

In conclusion, try and decide whether nature or nurture is more important in determining a person's characteristics.

_____

_____

_____

_____

Unit Adult decisions

The sorts of things that adults make decisions about as they develop are:

1. Starting a family
2. Buying/renting a house
3. Choice of job
4. Bringing up a family
5. Travel
6. Attitude to money e.g. saving up or buying on credit.

Read carefully the list of decisions that adults have to deal with. For each one, decide if the decision will be affected by physical, intellectual, emotional or social development. Write your conclusion in the spaces below and give reasons for your choice. You may find that some of the decisions are affected by more than one aspect.

1. Starting a family _____

_____

_____

2. Buying/renting a house _____

_____

_____

3. Choice of job _____

_____

_____

4. Starting a family _____

_____

_____

5. Travel _____

_____

_____

6. Attitude to money _____

_____

_____

Extension activity

▷ You are now within one year of being able to make some of those decisions yourself. What will you do when you have to make those decisions? At this stage you can plan without having to actually carry the plans out. Describe as fully as you can what decisions you will make about starting a family, buying/renting a house, etc. Be prepared to share your conclusions with the rest of the group.

Case study

Katherine was an only child. Her parents were keen to be 'good' parents and Katherine's mother who did not work, spent a lot of time with her when she was little. She was sent to play school when she was three, going three mornings a week. As a result, Katherine talked well at two years old and knew the alphabet and numbers up to ten before she went to school.

At primary school, Katherine settled in quickly. Although she had no sisters and brothers, her parents had encouraged her to mix with other children and she found school interesting and enjoyable. She quickly made friends. She managed to stay quite near the top of the class, although she could be a little lazy sometimes.

At eleven, she transferred to the local secondary school. There were a number of children from her primary school who also moved up with her, so at least she knew some other students before she started there. After the first couple of weeks, she began to settle down and made some new friends who had been at different primary schools. Her parents encouraged her to bring her friends home, so that they got to know them.

Katherine took her 'O' levels when she was 16. She got five above Grade C. Secretly, she knew that she could have done a lot better, but by then school bored her and she had done little revision, despite her parents' threats and bribes. They had wanted her to do 'A' levels and try for University but she had had enough of studying and so she chose a beauty course at the local college that included long periods of work experience in a salon, so that she didn't have to have to spend all her spare time studying.

When she was twenty, Katherine met Tony. He had been to the same college and had finished his course the year before Katherine. He was now working for a local builder and he was exciting and a 'good laugh'. They started going out together. Katherine took him home to meet her parents. The meeting was not a success. When he had gone home, her mother burst into tears! From then on, life at home became more and more difficult as her parents tried to persuade her to end the relationship. After one particularly bad row with them Katherine could stand it no longer and went to stay with a girlfriend. Two weeks later, she had found a flat and moved in with Tony.

By the time Katherine was thirty, she had two children aged three and five. She wasn't happy with Tony. Once she had had the children, he had lost interest in her. He had never seemed interested in the children at all. Katherine was extremely unhappy. She had given up her job at the salon once she was pregnant and had not returned. She still saw her friends from her college days and they regularly provided a shoulder to cry on. She had little money of her own and didn't see what she could do to get out of the mess that she felt that she was in.

Her parents were very concerned about her. They had never approved of Tony, but they loved their daughter and their grandchildren and could see that Katherine needed help. They suggested that Katherine moved back in with them so that they could look after the children, while she returned to college to gain some qualifications. In desperation, Katherine agreed.

Katherine went back to college and took her 'A' levels. She surprised herself by enjoying the work although she still didn't like living with her parents. After she passed her exams she applied for University and did a degree in social sciences so that she could become social worker. Finally after five years with her parents she was able to move out and support herself and the children on her salary as a social worker. She felt marvellous! Tony had made little attempt to see the children during this time and now just managed a card and present at Christmas and birthdays.

Unit 3 — Development of the individual (continued)

Case study (continued)

Three years later, Katherine married again. Her husband was called Tomas. He worked in the same office. They married six months after the first date. Katherine had always been impulsive, but this time her instincts were right. Tomas was a good stepfather to her children and they agreed that they did not want any more. They were both very keen on their careers and were promoted during the following five years.

Katherine is now retired. She lives with Tomas, near to her daughter so that they can visit her and the grandchildren regularly. Katherine goes to the local primary school every week to listen to the Y3 children read. She and Tomas are learning Spanish as they visit the country often on holiday. She still sees her friends each week, they laugh about the experiences that they have shared over the years they have known each other. Katherine now needs a hearing aid and if the weather is damp, suffers from arthritis in her knees but other than that, feels very well. She looks back at her life with satisfaction, she has had her problems but things turned out very well in the end.

Read the case study carefully and then answer the questions in your notes.

1. How did Katherine's mother help her develop intellectually as a baby?

2. How was Katherine encouraged to develop socially as a young child?

3. How did Katherine develop emotionally and socially during her childhood?

4. Describe Katherine's intellectual development during school and college.

5. Do you think Katherine developed emotionally and socially between the ages of twenty and thirty? Give reasons for your answer.

6. Describe Katherine's intellectual development during adulthood.

7. Describe Katherine's emotional and social development during adulthood.

8. How does Katherine continue to develop intellectually as an elderly person?

9. Describe Katherine's social and emotional development as an elderly person.

10. How has old age affected Katherine's physical development?

Worksheet 3.4
pages 168–169

A centile chart is a chart used by nurses and paediatricians (doctors specialising in the illnesses of children) to see if a child is growing at a normal rate for the child's age and sex.

The lower area of the page is used to measure weight. The higher area is used to measure height. When reading the chart, note that you read the child's height (in centimetres) from the left hand side of the chart and weight (in kilograms) from the right hand side of the page.

The heaviest line within the band indicates the normal height and weight for the child. This is called the **mid-line 50th centile**. The shaded areas below and above this line represent a height or weight where there would be medical concern and possible medical intervention. There are different charts for boys and girls.

Use the girls' 0–20 years median chart on page 118 to answer the following questions.

1. What is the normal average weight of a nine-year-old child?

    _____

2. What is the normal average height of a seven-year-old child?

    _____

3. What is the normal average weight of a child aged 12 years 6 months?

    _____

4. What is the normal average height of a child aged 11 years 6 months?

    _____

Extension activity

  1. Explain why a child aged nine who weighed 20 kgs would give cause for concern.

      _____

      _____

  2. Explain why a child aged 12 with a height of 167 cms would give cause for concern.

      _____

      _____

  3. State the weight ranges that would give cause for concern in 14-year-old girls.

      _____

      _____

Use the boys' 0–20 years median chart on page 118 to answer the following questions.

1. What is the normal average height of a 12-year-old boy?

_____

2. What is the normal average height of a 5-year-old boy?

_____

3. What is the normal average weight of a boy aged 15 years 6 months?

_____

4. What is the normal average height of a boy aged 14 years 6 months?

_____

Extension activity

▷ 1. State the height ranges that would give cause for concern in 16-year-old boys.

_____

_____

2. State the weight ranges that would give cause for concern in a boy aged 9 years 6 months.

_____

_____

3. Why would a boy aged 10 years old, who weighed 23 kgs, give cause for concern?

_____

_____

4. Why would a boy aged 12 years 6 months, who was 168 cms high, give cause for concern?

_____

_____

Unit 3 Using a centile chart

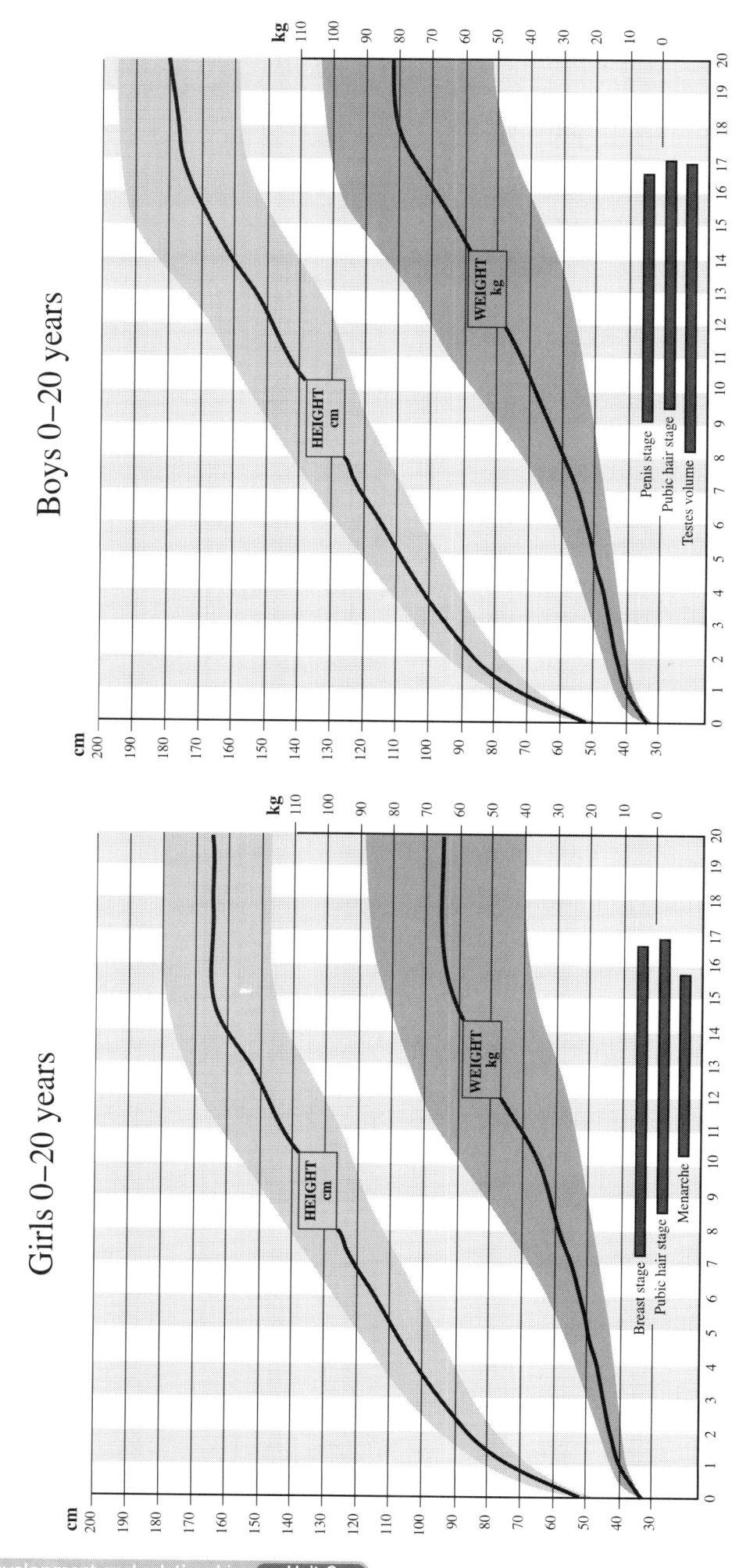

Boys 0–20 years

Girls 0–20 years

Unit **Earnings of men and women**

	Males		Females	
	Part-time	**Full-time**	**Part-time**	**Full-time**
1986	3.31	4.89	2.77	3.63
1988	3.56	5.74	3.22	3.63
1990	5.08	6.88	3.98	5.29
1992	5.69	8.07	4.74	6.40
1994	5.94	8.63	5.09	6.90
1996	6.52	9.33	5.44	7.51
1998	7.11	10.25	6.09	8.25
2000	7.66	11.00	6.75	9.02

Average gross hourly earnings (£/hour) for employees on adult rates in April each year.

(Source – New Earnings Survey. Crown copyright material is reproduced with the permission of the Controller of HMSO and the Queen's Printer for Scotland)

Draw a graph or use an application such as Excel to plot a graph to show men and women's full-time and part-time hourly earnings.

Now use the graph to answer the following questions.

1. Who earns more money, men or women?

_____

2. Who earns more money, part-time or full-time workers?

_____

3. Which group of workers has the greatest difference between their full-time and part-time hourly rates?

_____

4. Which group of workers have had the greatest increase in hourly rates between 1986 and 2000?

_____

Extension activity

▷ Use ideas you have covered in the course to explain why there are significant differences between the earnings of men and women.

_____

_____

_____

_____

 **Unit The effect of unemployment or retirement on health and well-being**

Worksheet 3.6
pages 187–188
and 236–237

Case study

Henry is 56 years old. He is married and lives with his wife, Mary. He had to retire from work as a sales manager three months ago and was not happy about it. The company had to cut down on employees and, because of his age, Henry was asked to go. He has got a pension, but it is not as good as it should have been because he had planned to work until he was 65 years old. If he had done so his pension would have been better. He feels lost at home and his wife says he is 'getting under her feet'.

Mary was not enjoying Henry's retirement

1. Identify and describe Henry and Mary's relationship. _____

_____

2. Why is Henry not happy about his retirement? _____

_____

3. What problems will he have in adjusting to retirement? _____

_____

4. What problems will Mary have in adjusting to Henry's retirement? _____

_____

5. How will retirement affect Henry's

   a) intellectual development? _____

   _____

   b) social development? _____

   _____

6. How will retirement affect the relationship between Henry and Mary? _____

_____

Extension activity

▷ 1. How will Henry's self-esteem be affected by retirement?

   _____

   _____

2. Imagine Henry is a relative of yours. What suggestions would you make to Henry to ensure that his personal development continues through retirement?

   _____

   _____

Unit 3 Living in a lone-parent family

1. What are the disadvantages for the parent and child of living in a lone-parent family?

2. What are the advantages for the parent and child?

3. Are there particular problems for girls living with Dad or boys living with Mum?

Discuss your ideas in small groups and list them on the page below. Then be ready to share your ideas with the class. Put the class conclusions in the space on this sheet.

Your group's ideas

_____
_____
_____
_____
_____
_____
_____
_____
_____

The class's ideas

_____
_____
_____
_____
_____
_____
_____
_____
_____

Extension activity

▷ Analyse the list of advantages and problems that you have identified in terms of the physical, intellectual, emotional and social development of the individual. For example, the close relationship that can develop between parent and child affects the child's emotional development.

Unit 3 Effect of life experiences on growth and development

Case study

Michael is 46 years old. The last year has been dreadful for him. He and his wife have divorced because she has fallen in love with another man. His ex-wife and the children have gone to live with him in another town. As part of the divorce settlement, the family home had to be sold so that the money from the house could be shared between the two of them. Michael feels very bitter about this, as he didn't want the divorce. He has had to move to a smaller house in an area where he doesn't know anyone yet. At work, there has been a fall in profits and rumours of redundancy keep passing around the office. To lose his job, on top of everything else that has happened, would be devastating.

1. Identify Michael's life stage. _____

2. List the risks to physical and mental health that Michael may experience as a result of the divorce.

_____

_____

_____

3. What problems may his children experience as a result of the divorce

    a) emotionally? _____

_____

    b) socially? _____

_____

4. What risks to his physical and mental health is Michael experiencing as a result of the situation at work? _____

_____

_____

5. What new risks may he suffer if he is made redundant? _____

_____

_____

Extension activity

▷ 1. Describe how the divorce will affect Michael's self-esteem.

_____

_____

   2. What effect will redundancy have on Michael's self-esteem?

_____

_____

Unit 3

The effect of divorce on the health and well-being of family members

Worksheet 3.9 pages 190 and 231

Case study

Mario and Linda are both in their early thirties and have two small children. They met when Linda went on holiday to Rimini with her friends. After they got married, they bought a house near Linda's mum. Mario has never felt at home in England. He hates the weather and misses his large family back in Italy. The couple have been arguing a lot lately and Linda is beginning to think that it would be better for the children if they separate and divorce. She has discussed the problem with her Mum, who has offered to let Linda and the children live with her if the marriage ends.

1. Identify the life stage of Mario and Linda. _____

2. What is Mario likely to do if the marriage ends? _____

_____

3. How is a divorce likely to affect the relationship that Mario has with his children?

_____

_____

4. How will a divorce affect the physical health and well-being of:

   a) the children? _____

   _____

   b) Linda? _____

   _____

   c) Linda's mum? _____

   _____

5. How will the divorce affect Linda's:

   a) emotional development? _____

   _____

   b) social development? _____

   _____

Extension activity

> 1. Mario and Linda come from different cultures. Explain the effect that could have had on their relationship.

_____

_____

2. If Linda and the children move in with her mother, what could be the effect on the relationships between the family members?

_____

_____

Case study

Sofia is fourteen. She lives with her two younger sisters and her parents. Her mother has Multiple Sclerosis, which has recently got worse. As a result she has been forced to use a wheelchair. Sofia's father works long hours at a local factory. This means that Sofia's mum is very dependent on Sofia to help her with the housework and look after the younger children. Sofia wants to help, as she feels very sorry for her mum, but is sometimes a bit resentful about how much she is asked to do.

1. Identify Sofia's life stage. _____

2. List the ways in which Sofia will be expected to help her Mum. _____

   _____

   _____

   _____

3. Sofia is one of her mother's main carers. How will this affect her:

   a) socially? _____

   _____

   b) intellectually? _____

   _____

   c) emotionally? _____

   _____

Extension activity

1. How will acting as her mother's carer affect Sofia's:

   a) self-esteem? _____

   _____

   _____

   b) mental health? _____

   _____

   _____

   c) level of education? _____

   _____

   _____

   d) employment prospects? _____

   _____

2. How will the situation affect her mother's self-esteem? _____

   _____

Unit 3 — The effect of diet on health and well-being

Case study

Hamish has recently lost his job on a building site. Since he has become unemployed, he has become depressed and bored. He has been eating far more food than he needs, so he has become overweight. He particularly likes chocolate bars between meals and bags of chips with gravy last thing in the evening. His weight increase has made him feel worse, so he eats more to cheer himself up! Hamish's friend Mike is becoming rather worried about him. He suggests that Hamish comes to five-a-side football with him at the local sports centre. Hamish feels embarrassed about his weight gain and is reluctant to go.

1. Identify and describe the type of relationship between Hamish and Mike.

_____

_____

2. Why would it be a good idea for Hamish to join Mike at the five-a-side?

_____

_____

3. How would it benefit his physical development? _____

_____

4. How would Hamish's social development be affected by joining Mike at the football?

_____

_____

5. What might happen to Hamish if he refuses to go with Mike?

_____

_____

6. Explain the effect on Hamish's physical health if he does not change his eating habits. (You could use information from Unit 2 to help you answer this question.)

_____

_____

_____

Extension activity

▷ 1. Explain how you think Hamish's weight gain is affecting his self-esteem.

_____

_____

2. What effect could this have on his employment prospects?

_____

_____

Living in poverty can have the following effects on people:

1. They will not be able to buy their children educational games or toys
2. They will have a poorer diet
3. They are more likely to be ill
4. They are less likely to have holidays
5. They are more likely to smoke
6. Their home may be small, cold or poorly furnished
7. Their social life may be limited by their lack of money
8. Lack of money may prevent them from using sports facilities e.g. the local swimming pool.

Read the effects of having a low income. Now list the **consequences** of a low income for an individual. For example, the consequence of being unable to buy a child educational toys could be that a child will do less well at school.

Explain how each consequence that you name will affect the physical, intellectual, emotional or social development of an individual.

1. _____
2. _____
3. _____
4. _____
5. _____
6. _____
7. _____
8. _____

Extension activity

▷ Explain clearly how poverty can affect:

a) The self-esteem of the individual _____
_____

b) Level of education _____
_____
_____
_____

c) Employment opportunities _____
_____
_____

Unit 3 Marriages and divorces

Worksheet 3.13
pages 189–190
and page 210

Marriages and divorces in the UK (thousands)

Year	First marriages	Divorces	Remarriages
1961	340	27	57
1971	369	79	91
1981	263	175	135
1991	222	174	127
1999	179	159	122

(Source – Marriages and divorces 1961–1999. Crown copyright material is reproduced with the permission of the Controller of HMSO and the Queen's Printer for Scotland.)

1. Use a computer program such as Excel or use graph paper to draw a bar chart of the statistics above.

2. Describe the pattern that you see in the numbers of marriages. _____
   _____

3. Describe the pattern that you see in the numbers of divorces. _____
   _____

4. Use the bar chart to estimate the number of marriages in 2011 if the trend continues in the same pattern. _____
   _____

5. The number of divorces seems to be falling. Using the bar chart, can you explain why?
   _____
   _____
   _____

Extension activity

1. Use ideas from Chapter 12 to explain **why** the number of marriages is falling.
   _____
   _____

2. Use ideas from Chapter 12 to explain **why** the divorce rate increased between 1961 and 1981.
   _____
   _____

3. Couples who do not marry often **co-habit** instead.

   (a) What is co-habitation? _____
   _____

   (b) Why do you think couples choose to co-habit instead of marrying? _____
   _____

   (c) What are the disadvantages for children of couples who co-habit? _____
   _____

Case study

Louise lives with her three-year-old son, Kyle, in a council flat on the tenth floor of a tower block. She has no job, as she cannot afford to pay for childcare, so she lives on state benefits. Her parents live on the other side of town and have no car. This means that she can only visit them if she uses the bus, as they cannot come for her. Louise hates the flat. She sees little of her neighbours and there is nowhere for Kyle to play so that he can become very irritable because he has to stay inside most of the time. The lift to the flat is often broken which means just going to the shops can be difficult because they have to walk up and down the stairs. Louise would like a little house with a garden near her family but the Council have told her that it will take some time before one becomes available for her.

1. Identify and describe the relationship of Kyle and Louise. _____

_____

2. Describe how Kyle's environment will affect his physical development.

_____

_____

3. How will Kyle's home affect his:

a) emotional development? _____

_____

b) social development? _____

_____

c) intellectual development? _____

_____

4. Describe in terms of the PIES how Louise and Kyle's health and well-being would improve if they were able to move to a house with a garden near to her parents.

_____

_____

_____

Extension activity

▷ 1. Describe the effect of living in the flat on Louise's self-esteem. _____

_____

_____

2. Explain how her self-esteem could change as a result of the move to a more pleasant home environment. _____

_____

_____

Unit 3 Gender issues

Margaret Thatcher was Britain's first female Prime Minister. Elaine Griffiths is one of only three female cardiac (heart) surgeons in Britain. What difficulties do you think these women overcame to achieve so much in traditionally male occupations? You could identify the problems that they had to overcome in terms of the PIES.

Physical difficulties _____

_____

_____

_____

Intellectual difficulties _____

_____

_____

_____

Emotional difficulties _____

_____

_____

_____

Social difficulties _____

_____

_____

_____

Extension activity

▷ Imagine you are the only male employee among a group of women or the only female employee among a group of men.

1. How would you overcome the type of problems that you have identified above?

    _____

    _____

    _____

2. How would the situation affect your self-esteem? Give reasons for your answer.

    _____

    _____

    _____

Case study

Mrs Zabci and her four-year-old son Faruk are asylum seekers who have come to live in Britain. Mrs Zabci hoped to go and live in London with friends but she has been sent to a large Northern city where she has been allocated a flat in a tower block. She has vouchers that she can exchange for food and £10 per week in cash. Mrs Zabci's English is very limited and she feels very isolated in the flat. A man from the Council comes to see her each week to make sure that she is all right, but other than this, Mrs Zabci has little contact with other people. She is now very worried because her son seems to be unwell, he has complained of the cold and he has a cough that doesn't seem to be clearing up.

1. Identify the life stages of Mrs Zabci and her son Faruk. _____

_____

2. Describe the aspects of Mrs Zabci's situation that mean that she is unlikely to gain good access to the health and welfare services that she needs.

_____

_____

_____

_____

_____

3. Describe how Mrs Zabci's situation will affect her:

a) social development _____

_____

_____

b) emotional development _____

_____

_____

Extension activity

▷ 1. Faruk will soon start school. Explain how his home circumstances will affect his chances of educational success. _____

_____

_____

2. Describe how her home circumstances will affect Mrs Zabci's self-esteem.

_____

_____

_____

1.
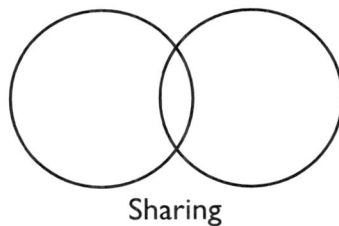
Sharing

2.
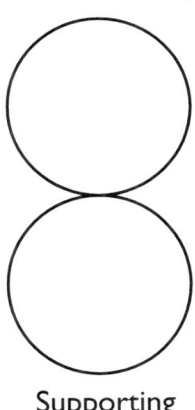
Supporting

3.
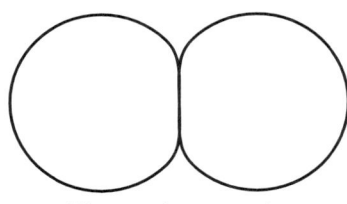
Physical attraction

4.
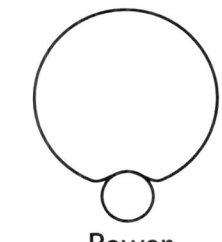
Power

5.
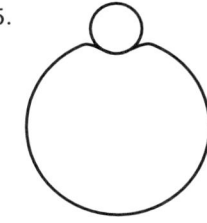
Dependency

The diagrams above represent types of relationships.

1. For each type, give as many suggestions as you can of different examples of the relationship e.g. three single girls may share a flat. This is an example of a sharing relationship. A middle-aged man may regularly visit his elderly neighbour to make sure he is all right. This is a supporting relationship.

_____

_____

_____

_____

_____

_____

2. Relationships change over time. For example, a child is dependent on her parents but as an adult may act as a support when her parents become elderly. Now suggest how the relationships you identified above can change over time to another type.

_____

_____

_____

_____

_____

3. Relationships can be either **positive** or **negative**. Decide which of the relationships that you have already identified are positive or negative.

_____

_____

_____

_____

_____

_____

Extension activity

▷ 1. Some negative relationships become **abusive**. From the work you have done in this unit, suggest the types of relationships that can become abusive.

_____

_____

_____

_____

2. Give reasons to explain why relationships can become abusive.

_____

_____

_____

_____

3. What is the effect on the personal development of young children who have been abused? You could describe the effects in terms of the PIES.

_____

_____

_____

_____

Case study

Elizabeth is 76 years old. She has lived alone since her husband died three years ago. She has only one son, Callum who lives nearby. Callum is married to Diane. Elizabeth and Diane have never really got on since the wedding when Diane overheard Elizabeth tell one of her friends that she was disappointed in Callum's choice of a wife. Callum and Diane have two sons. Elizabeth finds them very noisy and she particularly dislikes the clothes they choose to wear. She believes that Callum and Diane are too 'soft' with them and does not hesitate to tell Callum this regularly.

1. Identify Elizabeth's life stage. _____

2. Do you think Elizabeth will have a good relationship with her daughter-in-law and grandchildren? Give reasons for your answer. _____

_____

_____

3. What can Callum do about his mother's attitude to his family? _____

_____

_____

4. What do you think will happen if Elizabeth needs help from her son and his family in the future? _____

_____

_____

5. Do you think Elizabeth will have a positive or negative relationship with her grandsons? Give reasons for your answer. _____

_____

_____

6. How will Elizabeth's relationship with her son's family affect her self-esteem?

_____

_____

Extension activity

▷ 1. How do you think Elizabeth's attitude to the family will affect the relationship between Callum and Diane? Give reasons for your answer. _____

_____

2. If Elizabeth became ill and came to live with the family, the relationship could become **abusive**. Explain why this is a possibility. _____

_____

_____

Unit The 'rules' of friendship

There are 'rules' which close friends will obey so that friendships will continue. The 'rules' of close friendship state that:

1. A friend stands up for another person if they are not there
2. You should share good news with a friend
3. A friend will provide support when things are not going well
4. Friends trust and confide in each other
5. Friends volunteer help to their friend
6. Friends try to please each other when they are in each other's company.

1. Think of the person whom you consider to be your closest friend. Read again the list of rules of close friendship. Taking each one in turn, describe examples of occasions when your friend has followed the rules during the time you have been friendly.

Rule 1. _____

Rule 2. _____

Rule 3. _____

Rule 4. _____

Rule 5. _____

Rule 6. _____

2. Describe the effect on you when a person that you considered to be a good friend has broken the 'rules'. _____

_____

_____

_____

_____

Extension activity

▷ 1. Friendship is essential to help you develop as a person. Use examples to describe how your friendships helped you to develop:

    a) Socially _____

_____

    b) Emotionally _____

_____

2. Give examples to explain how your friends affect your self-esteem:

    a) Positively _____

_____

    b) Negatively _____

_____

Unit 3

The effect of sexual orientation on the self-concept

Case study

Ian is a nurse in a large city hospital. He has known that he is gay since he was about fifteen. He did not discuss his sexuality with anyone until he started nursing. Then it seemed easy to discuss it and his colleagues have always accepted him. However he has still not discussed it with anyone at home. He tried to raise the subject with his sister but she made some rude comments about gays and he changed the subject quickly. His Dad always makes tasteless comments if actors or singers known to be gay come on the TV. Ian loves his family and would like to tell them the truth about himself but he is very worried about what their reaction will be.

1. Identify and describe the relationship between Ian and his sister. _____

_____

_____

2. Identify and describe the relationship Ian has with the other nurses at the hospital.

_____

_____

_____

3. How will the reaction of Ian's colleagues affect his self-concept? _____

_____

_____

_____

4. How will the comments of his family affect his self-concept? _____

_____

_____

_____

5. Whose comments do you think will have the greater affect on Ian? Give reasons for your answer. _____

_____

_____

_____

6. How could the comments of his family affect Ian's emotional development?

_____

_____

_____

Extension activity

▷ Eventually Ian is likely to form a relationship with another man. He will either finally have to tell his parents the truth about his sexuality or keep the relationship secret. Both outcomes will affect his relationship with his partner.

1. How will the relationship with his partner be affected if:

   a) He keeps the relationship secret? _____

   _____

   _____

   b) He tells his parents? _____

   _____

   _____

2. If he tells his parents the truth about himself, how will this affect his:

   a) Self-esteem? _____

   _____

   _____

   b) Self-concept? _____

   _____

   _____

The game board (snakes and ladders) contains the following squares and labels:

Happiness! (If you don't feel happy go back to 53) **99**	**98** Unemployment Go back 4 spaces	**97** Redundancy Go back 10 spaces	**96**	**95** **94** Success in Education approach gain 2 turns **92** **91**
81	**82** **83** Compatible	**84** **77** Friendship	**85** Serious illness **76** Aware of own emotions **88**	**89** You find love Go forward 3 spaces **90**
Poor communication Skills Go back 5 Spaces **80**	**79** Reduced life chances Miss a turn Bereavement **62 63** relationship	Being alone Miss a turn **75**	**73** Divorce **74** **67 68** Self-confidence	Change in life Miss a turn **72 71**
You get a good job Go forward 7 spaces **61**	**60 59**	**58 57** **64 65 66** Stress and worry	Fall out with a friend Miss a turn **56 55 54** you are **53** **48 49** Good self-concept	**69 70** community and you feel you belong **52 51**
Learning from older children when young gain a turn **41 42**	**40** **39** Good economic environment	**43** **38 37** You think you are unattractive Advance to Square 53 No	feeling of who **36 35** supportive carers **46 47** Negative self-concept **34 27**	change in life Miss a turn **50** Stress Go back 7 spaces **31 32** Sense of self worth **29**
21	**22 23** Difficult family relationships	**24 18 17**	Family arguments Go back 1 space **25** feeling you are a failure Go back 7 spaces **44 45**	**30 28** **11**
Your carers value education 2 extra turns **20**	**19**	Loving parents Move 7 spaces on **2 3**	**16 14** Supportive family Gain a turn **15 13 12**	
START 1		**4** caring friendship	Parents argue and are stressed Miss a turn **5 6**	**7 8 9 10**

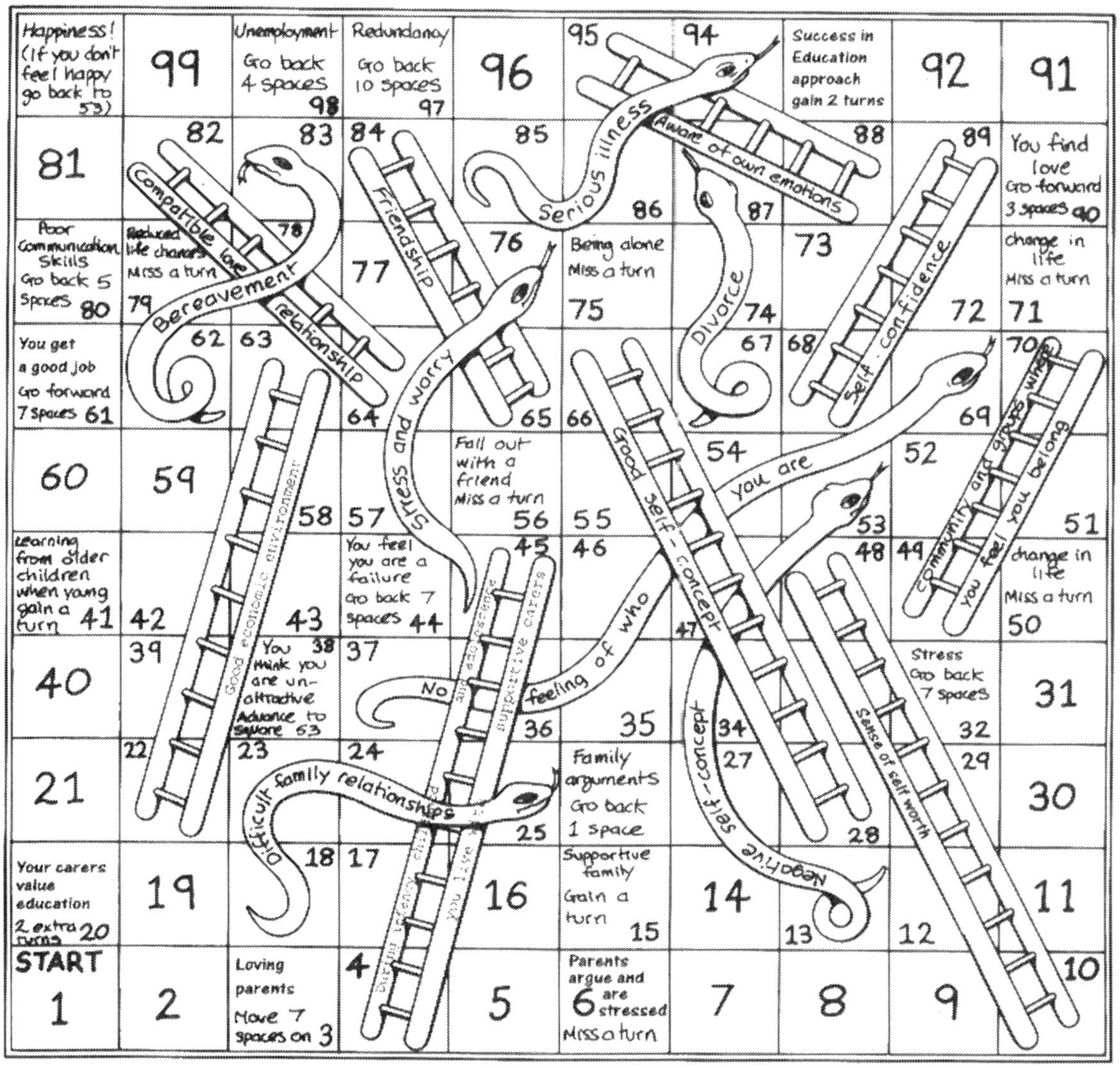

Discuss how the ups and downs in life can affect how a person understands himself or herself.

Make two counters and play the game of 'Self-concept snakes and ladders'. At each snake or ladder, discuss with your partner the effect that the factor would have on your self-concept.

Extension activity

▷ Take each example of factors that affect the self-concept and explain the positive and negative effect that they can have.

_____

_____

_____

_____

Unit 3 — Obtaining help from professional carers and services

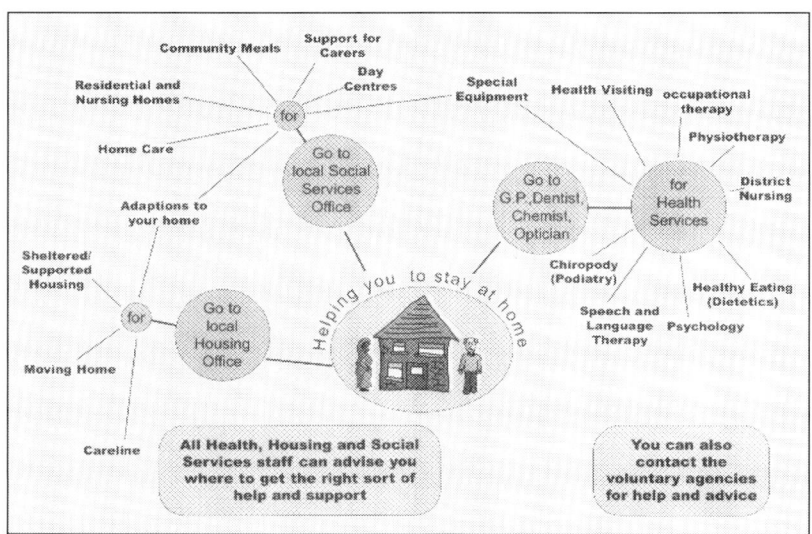

Use the diagram above to explain the ways in which it is possible for the people in the case studies below to obtain help and support from professional services. In some cases, more than one type of support may be needed. You may find that there is more than one way of obtaining help.

Case study 1

Your grandmother is physically weak, but mentally very well. She needs adaptation to her bathroom to enable her to wash herself and a walking frame to help her get around the house. She has leg ulcers that need regular treatment.

Case study 2

Your child is physically and mentally handicapped. He requires a new wheelchair, as he gets bigger. He also needs help to improve his speech. Your home needs a ramp to the front door to enable you to get the wheelchair in and out. You feel you need some advice to help you care for your child and the problems that his care involves.

Case study 3

Your elderly mother lives with you. She is lonely and needs the company of people her own age. You are not able to take her out as you work full time. She is physically able except for a large bunion on her foot that is painful and requires regular treatment.

Case study 4

Your husband has had a car accident. He will eventually recover but will have a long recuperation time at home. He needs nursing care to deal with his injuries and physiotherapy to help the muscles in his legs. While he recovers, he could do with some company during the day, while you are at work.

Unit Guidance for the assessment

Unit 1: How to write your report

You need to produce a report of your investigation into local providers of health, social care or early years services. The list below explains the breadth of your task, based on your particular exam board. Your teacher will tell which exam board specification you are following.

AQA:	At least two local providers of health, social care or early years services, used by two people from different client groups, for example a nursery and a residential care setting, providing services for children of nursery age and people over a particular age or with a particular need respectively.
Edexcel:	One local provider of health, social care or early years services, used by two different clients with different needs, for example, a nursery which runs a before school club, providing services for children of nursery age and of primary school age.
OCR:	Two local providers of health, social care or early years services used by people in the area, for example, a nursery and a residential care setting.

Whichever board you are using, the following guidance will help you to put your assignments together. The headings and sections are only suggestions. Remember that the more relevant detail you include, the higher the grade you will hopefully achieve. You can collect much of the information needed by visiting the service/s you pick and completing the work placement diary which your teacher will have had printed for you.

It is very important that throughout your assignment you use and identify as many sources of information as possible. You also need to include as many examples from real life as you can in each section.

N.B. These notes assume that more than one service is being written about in the assignment. You will need to bear this in mind if you only need to base your assignment on one provider.

Introduction

This should include details about the care settings you have chosen to base your assignment on, such as:

✓ the type of service provision i.e. health, social care or early years or a mixture of these
✓ addresses
✓ the days and hours it is available
✓ the sector they fall into i.e. public, private, voluntary or not-for-profit
✓ a population profile of your local area
✓ the sources of funding at local and national level which allow the services to be provided
✓ how funding at national and local levels affects the provision of services
✓ any variation in funding locally for each service in comparison with national provision, with reasons; for example, a particular service might be more heavily funded in an inner city area because there is more demand for it than there is in a rural area
✓ how the local services you have chosen fit into the national framework – you could draw a diagram for this with brief notes to explain it
✓ how the targets set for the services you have chosen compare and contribute towards the government health targets
✓ how the funding is linked to those targets.

Remember to clearly state the source of your information. If you use more than one source of information, for example, visiting the place and talking to people there, leaflets, the Internet etc. you will get more marks, so it is important that they are all listed.

The needs of the people using the services

This section needs to include the following information:

✓ identify the physical, psychological, intellectual, emotional and social needs for the client groups which use the services chosen - this could be done using a survey
✓ how the services are organised to meet their needs
✓ how the services are delivered
✓ how well the services meet the needs of local people – again this could be done by conducting a survey

- ✓ your conclusion about how the needs of people are being met or not
- ✓ how the needs of people might change over time
- ✓ how the services cope with this changing need
- ✓ identify any gaps that exist in the services
- ✓ suggest improvements that could be made in the provision of services
- ✓ show that you understand the need for services to work together to fully meet the needs of clients and that these needs may be met by different organisations or sectors.

The roles of the care workers

This section should include details such as:

- ✓ an accurate description of the jobs done by the care workers, including day-to-day tasks
- ✓ how the activities and skills of the care workers enable the needs of the clients to be met, including non-physical needs
- ✓ how the activities the care workers do link with the level of responsibility of the care worker, such as which care workers are allowed to give medication and which are not
- ✓ the qualifications needed by the care workers
- ✓ the routes taken by the care workers to get their qualifications, knowledge and skills
- ✓ the qualities the care workers need, such as being a good listening
- ✓ alternative routes they could have taken to get the qualifications, such as learning on the job instead of going to college
- ✓ the advantages and disadvantages of each route.

Again, remember to identify clearly your sources of information.

The care value base

This section should include:

- ✓ a description of what is meant by the care value base
- ✓ a list of all the main features of the care value base
- ✓ examples of ways in which the care workers in your chosen services use different parts of the care value base in their day-to-day tasks (list as many examples as you can think of)
- ✓ a comparison of the ways in which care workers providing different services apply the care value base, giving similarities and differences
- ✓ an explanation of how it will affect the clients if the care workers do not apply the care value base
- ✓ examples of the possible conflicts care workers face when promoting values such as the rights of individuals, for example, when a care worker

is looking after someone who has different religious beliefs from themselves that affect how they care for that client, such as not being allowed to give blood to a Jehovah's Witness.

Codes of practice and charters

This section needs to include:

- ✓ a list of the codes of practice and charters used by your chosen services
- ✓ copies of some of these if you can get hold of them
- ✓ an explanation of how these are used by your services to help to meet the needs of the clients
- ✓ similarities and differences between those used by each service
- ✓ how these affect the standard of care provided for clients by your chosen services.

Referral to services

This section needs to include:

- ✓ details of different ways in which people can access the services they need
- ✓ details of the range of things that may stop people obtaining services, i.e. barriers such as physical, geographical, psychological etc.
- ✓ details of the communication skills needed by care workers
- ✓ an explanation as to why care workers need effective communication skills
- ✓ an explanation of any barriers to communication that may arise
- ✓ an explanation of how these barriers to communication can be overcome
- ✓ examples to illustrate your points regarding access to local services experienced by individuals
- ✓ an evaluation of the effectiveness of relevant procedures, i.e. how easy or difficult it is to access services and why you think this
- ✓ your realistic suggestions (at least three) as to how access to services can be improved i.e. how barriers to services can be overcome
- ✓ a description of the implications of widening access to services to local and national provision
- ✓ an explanation as to why being able to access services can empower people, for example, being able to get advice from social services on how to claim money can enable a client to afford a better lifestyle and so lead to improved health and well-being.

Remember to identify your sources of information, including those who actually use the services, although you must ask permission to use their names. If this is not given you must use a fictitious (made up) name.

Unit 2: How to write a health plan

You need to produce a health plan for improving or maintaining the physical health and well-being of one individual. The individual can be you, one of your friends or a member of your family. **Worksheet 2.10** will help you to pick your individual.

AQA: Your plan must include (a) defining the health and well-being of the individual; (b) factors affecting the health and well-being of the individual; (c) risks to the individual's health; (d) records of the use of two measures of health for the chosen individual; (e) changes the plan might have on the individual.

Edexcel: Your plan must (a) include an explanation of what is meant by health and well-being; (b) identify factors which have both a good and bad effect on an individual's health and well-being, and explain the effect these factors have; (c) identify appropriate information to set targets and measures of health for the individual; (d) include an assessment of how the plan may affect the individual, together with an evaluation of the difficulties which may be met in following and achieving the plan and how these difficulties may be overcome.

OCR: Your plan must cover: (a) defining the health and well-being of the individual; (b) factors that positively affected the individual's health and well-being; (c) risks to the individual's health and well-being; (d) interpreting physical measures of health for the individual; (e) ways in which the individual can be motivated and supported to maintain or improve their health and well-being.

The following notes will help you to put together your plan. Remember that the more relevant detail you include, and the more sections you complete, the higher your mark will be. It is a good idea to illustrate your assignment to make it look more attractive. You should also use a clear layout with lots of headings to break up the text. There are many free leaflets about health and well-being which you can use for both information and illustrations. Make sure you state your sources of information in each section.

Introduction

This should be a case study of your chosen person i.e. a description of your person and their lifestyle, in as much detail as possible. Interview the person and write up the results of the interview. This could be in the form of questions and answers, as a series of bullet points or even as a passport style profile. This should give an idea of how the individual views his or her own state of physical, intellectual, emotional and social health and well-being.

Your case study should contain the following information:

✓ name of the individual (or a false name if they would rather)
✓ family details
✓ height, weight and build
✓ age
✓ occupation
✓ working hours
✓ what they do in their spare time
✓ if they smoke and/or drink; how many cigarettes they smoke/how much they drink a day or week
✓ a description of their personality e.g. quiet and shy, bubbly and outgoing
✓ any additional information such as their culture, the environment they live in etc. that might affect their health and well-being.

It would also be a good idea to include a photograph of your person.

Health and well-being

You need to give as many different definitions of health and well-being as you can, writing accurately and clearly.

- ✓ Include examples to show that you understand what you are writing about
- ✓ Show that you understand the difference between positive and negative descriptions
- ✓ Show clearly how definitions have changed over time
- ✓ Make sure you include a holistic definition of health and well-being including physical, intellectual, emotional and social needs
- ✓ Relate these needs to your chosen person to give a detailed interpretation of their physical, intellectual, emotional and social health status.

Factors that affect [.......'s] health and well-being

You need to insert your chosen person's name in the heading. Then *list* and *explain in as much detail as possible*, the different factors that affect health and well-being, including how each factor affects the body both in the short and long term. You should include:

- ✓ all factors that have a positive effect on your person, such as eating a balanced diet (this could be sub-headed **positive factors**)
- ✓ all factors that have a negative effect on your person, such as smoking or drinking (this could be sub-headed **risks to health**). This could include an analysis of a day's diet, using appropriate software, to show that they don't eat enough of a particular food group and too much of another
- ✓ how these factors have worked together to affect your person; for example, how drinking in the pub with others who smoke a lot has led to them smoking more than they used to and has limited the exercise they can do due to respiratory difficulties brought on by smoking
- ✓ the theories or opinions of others who know the person as to how these factors have influenced your chosen person.

Make sure you list all your sources of information

Measures of health

You need to describe *in as much detail as possible* measures of health such as:

- ✓ height and weight charts
- ✓ body mass index
- ✓ peak flow

- ✓ blood pressure
- ✓ resting pulse and recovery after exercise

For each one describe:

- ✓ what the measure of health actually measures
- ✓ how it is measured
- ✓ how it is used i.e. a comparison with accepted standard data such as the safe ranges of blood pressure, the dangerous values of BMI etc.
- ✓ the measures of health for your chosen person (as many as possible, but at least two)

Compare their results against the norms of development, to be found in Chapter 9 of the GCSE Health and Social Care textbook. For each it would be a good idea to have a picture or photograph of the equipment needed to take these measurements, and photos of your chosen person using the equipment if possible

Choose two of the measures of health and say why you feel they will be most useful to your person and why the others would be less useful or inappropriate

Targets

- ✓ You need to look at all the information you have gathered so far and list that which will help you set targets to help improve the health and well-being of your chosen person, such as the number of cigarettes they smoke a day, or an analysis of their diet which might show that they eat too many fatty foods.
- ✓ Use the information to suggest short and long-term targets. These must be appropriate and realistic, e.g.

Short-term target	cut down on drinking during the week (you can make exact suggestions as to quantity, depending on your person's drinking habits),
Long-term target	cut out alcohol altogether except on special occasions

- ✓ Try to set targets for physical, intellectual, social and emotional effects.

Health plan

- ✓ You need to produce a detailed plan that should be laid out clearly, attractively and accurately so that your person can pick it up at home, understand it and follow it. For example, you could produce a table, with the risks to health down one side e.g. smoking, and actual time periods, e.g. immediately, two weeks, a month, six months and a year, across the top to give some short and longer term targets.

✓ Write notes for your person saying how they can stick to the plan and how it will help them if they stick to it.

✓ Include your sources of information so that they know where to look if they want more information or guidance.

Analysis of my plan

This should include:

✓ how you think the plan will affect your person, e.g. feeling more alert straight away if they give up drinking and allowing their liver to regenerate in the longer term, thereby reducing the risk of disease such as sclerosis of the liver

✓ include physical, intellectual, emotional and social effects

✓ reasons why your person should stick to the plan

✓ what difficulties you think your person will have in trying to stick to the plan, such as being tempted to drink when out with their friends

✓ suggestions as to how your person might overcome these difficulties, such as asking her/his friends to only buy her/him soft drinks

✓ the changes that will have the most impact on the person's health and well-being if they are successful in sticking to the plan

✓ why you think these changes will have the most effect

✓ at which stage in the plan each change will make a significant effect

✓ suggestions for alternatives when your person is in a position where it is hard to do as you have suggested in the plan, for example, how to cope when going out for a meal on a special occasion when your person is on a diet

It would be a good idea if you could give the plan to your person and ask them to write a statement for your portfolio saying how realistic and useful the plan is or isn't. If their statement is not very supportive statement, you could produce a new plan based on the comments made and repeat the process. You could even ask your person to stick to the plan for as long as possible and get them to describe the effects your plan has had on them.

Remember: More detail, more sources of information, more clear planning and layout = more marks!

Unit 3 Guidance for the assessment

Practice exam papers and marking schemes

Please note that the following practice exam papers and mark schemes are not intended to replicate an actual examination but to provide examination practice for Unit 3. The suggested answers and marking schemes are supplied by the authors and are not the responsibility of the awarding body.

For further guidance on assessment, it is recommended that teachers consult the Edexcel, OCR and AQA websites.

1   The following table gives some key features of development in the five life stages. Complete the table. The first one has been done for you.

Key feature	Life stage
Breasts develop	Adolescence
Learns to talk	
Retirement	
Understands and follows rules when playing a game	
Starts to walk	
The menopause occurs	

(5 marks)

2   a)   Personal development can be described in terms of physical development, intellectual development, emotional development and social development. Identify the type of development that occurs in each of the life changes below.

Life change	Type of development
Starting work	
Death of parents	
Periods begin	
Getting married	
Going to college	
Making friends at school	

(6 marks)

b)   Identify **two** examples of physical skills acquired by babies.

_____

_____

c)   Identify **two** examples of intellectual skills acquired by babies.

_____

_____

d)   Identify **two** examples of physical development in adolescents.

_____

_____

(6 marks)

3   Susan is fifteen. She lives with her two elder brothers and her Dad. Her Mum died three years ago. The family live in a small, rented house, which tends to get very untidy. The family do not have a lot of money. Susan is getting rather overweight. The family eats a lot of take-away food, as no one likes cooking. Susan feels she needs some advice about her weight but the GP's surgery is a bus ride away. Susan is reluctant to talk to her Dad about her weight and lacks confidence to go to see the doctor on her own.

a) What effect is Susan's weight having on her **self-esteem**?

_____

_____

(2 marks)

b) What effect could her weight gain have on:

   i) Her **physical health**? _____

_____

   ii) Her **mental health** _____

_____

(4 marks)

c) Susan is the only girl in the family. Use ideas about **gender** to explain how this will affect her relationships with other family members.

_____

_____

_____

(2 marks)

d) Give reasons why Susan has poor access to **health and welfare services**.

_____

_____

_____

(3 marks)

e) Explain how Susan's poor access to **health and welfare services** will affect her **physical** health.

_____

_____

_____

(3 marks)

4 People have different **types** of relationships.

- Family
- Friendships
- Intimate and sexual
- Working

a) Identify the **type** of relationship that is described below.

Description of relationship	Type of relationship
Two single girls plan a holiday together	
An elderly man collects his grandson from school	
A young couple decide to start a family	
A laboratory technician discusses the chemical stock with his line manager	

(4 marks)

Relationships that go wrong can become **abusive**. Describe why the following relationships could become **abusive**.

b) An elderly woman who is physically very weak comes to live with her daughter. Her daughter has two children and a demanding job.

_____

_____

_____

(2 marks)

c) A lone parent has three children and no job. Her middle child does not sleep well and is hard to discipline.

_____

_____

_____

(2 marks)

5   Michael is seventeen and lives with his parents and younger sister. His father drinks heavily and is then abusive to his mother. Michael hates his father for this behaviour but feels powerless to stop it, as his father is much bigger than him. Michael works in a garage. He gets on well with the other mechanics. They often go out together on a Friday evening. His boss is called Mr Stevens. He is strict with the mechanics and makes sure they work hard. Michael's girlfriend is called Emma. She is a hairdressing apprentice. Michael has been going out with her since they were at school.

a) The relationship Michael has with his father is a **negative** one. Describe the effect this will have on Michael's personal development.

_____

_____

_____

_____

_____

(2 marks)

b) The relationship he has with Emma is **positive**. What effect will this have on Michael's personal development?

_____

_____

_____

_____

_____

(3 marks)

c) He has a **positive** relationship with the mechanics at work. What effect will this have on his personal development?

_____

_____

_____

_____

_____

(3 marks)

d) Michael's mother has decided to leave his father and get a divorce. This is an **unexpected life event**. Describe what **professional carers and services** there are available to her at this difficult time.

_____

_____

_____

_____

(3 marks)

e) Describe what **faith-based support** there may be available to help Michael's mother.

_____

_____

_____

(2 marks)

f) Explain how **friends and family** can provide support for Michael's mother as she goes through the divorce.

_____

_____

_____

_____

(3 marks)

6 Self-concept is a term used to describe the way a person thinks of themselves. It is made up of **self-image** and **self-esteem**.

Sofiyah is 15. She has an older brother, Amit, who is 24. They both still live with their parents. The family is quite well off. Sofiyah feels that Amit is her parents 'favourite'. Her parents often talk about the grandchildren they will have when Amit marries and has a family. Amit has a very good job as an accountant. He is homosexual but feels unable to tell his parents about this. Sofiyah is very bright and wants to go to a good university so that she can become a barrister. Her parents are not very supportive of these plans. She is being bullied by a small group of girls at the school she attends.

a) What is meant by **self-image**?

_____

_____

(1 mark)

b) What is meant by **self-esteem?**

_____

_____

(1 mark)

c) Describe the **physical** factors that will affect the self-concept of both Amit and Sofiyah.

_____

_____

_____

(4 marks)

d) Identify and describe how **intellectual** factors will affect the self-concept of
i) Amit and ii) Sofiyah

_____

_____

_____

_____

_____

_____

(6 marks)

e) Identify and describe how **emotional** factors will affect the self-concept of i) Amit and
ii) Sofiyah.

_____

_____

_____

_____

_____

_____

(8 marks)

f) Identify and describe how **social** factors will affect Sofiyah's self-concept.

_____

_____

_____

_____

_____

(3 marks)

7 The following **life events** can have an effect on the personal development of the
individual. Complete the table to identify which are **expected** and which are **unexpected**
life events.

Life event	Expected or unexpected
Marriage	
Leaving home	
Redundancy	
Retirement	
Serious car accident	
Puberty	
Death of a sibling	

(7 marks)

Total: 85 marks

Practice marking scheme for Edexcel

1   Infancy
Later adulthood
Childhood
Infancy
Adulthood
1 mark per answer = 5 marks

2   **a)**   Type of development
Intellectual
Emotional
Physical
Emotional
Intellectual
Social
1 mark per answer = 6 marks

b)   Control of head/gross motor skills
Control of limbs
Control of fingers/manipulative skills/fine motor skills
Walking/standing/running
(any 2)
2 marks

c)   Talking
Recognising or carrying out gestures e.g. waving good-bye
Playing simple games e.g. peek-a-boo
Carrying out simple skills e.g. completing jigsaws
(any 2)
2 marks

d)   Development of sexual characteristics
Breasts develop
Penis enlarges
Growth of pubic hair
Body changes in shape e.g. hips get bigger in girls, shoulders get wider in boys
Voice breaks in boys
(any 2)
2 marks

Total: 6 marks

3   **a)**   Lowering her self-esteem/as teenagers are concerned about their appearance.
2 marks

b)   **i)**   Physical health – increased risk of wear on joints/potential problems with heart and circulation system.
ii)   Mental health – anxiety/due to worries about appearance
4 marks

c)   May feel left out
May feel she has to 'look after' the others
May feel special as she is the only girl
May feel she has no one to talk to
(any 2)
2 marks

d)   Long distance to the GP/would need to use public transport.
Lacks confidence to speak to GP on her own/is embarrassed to talk to parent who could take her

She is young – doesn't feel able to approach the health professionals
(any 3)
3 marks

e) Unable to get the advice she needs/therefore she will not have information to change her eating habits and eat more healthily.
3 marks

Total: 14 marks

4 a) Friendship
Family
Intimate and sexual
Working
4 marks

b) Daughter has a lot to cope with/may become impatient with elderly, dependant parent who needs help
2 marks

c) Parent is already under stress/may not know the appropriate way to care for the child/may not like the child (because of his behaviour)
2 marks

5 a) Will feel inadequate
Bad atmosphere in the home
Poor role model
Lowered self-esteem
(any)
2 marks

b) Feels love from/towards her
Good relationship aids self-esteem/self-confidence
Someone to confide in
Someone to spend time with, away from his home
(any)
3 marks

c) Good working relationships/make work more enjoyable
Someone to talk to
Improve his social life
Improve self-esteem
(any)
3 marks

d) GP
Relate/counselling services
Social services
Housing department
Social Security
(any)
3 marks

e) Local church/vicar/priest
Support groups/counselling associated with the church
2 marks

f) Someone to talk to
May lend money to help out
May let her stay when she leaves
May help to find somewhere to live
May help her move possessions
(any)
3 marks

6 a) How you see yourself as a person/outward facing
1 mark

b) What you think about yourself/self-confidence/inward facing
1 mark

c) Enough money
Comfortable home
2 marks
Effect on self-concept – secure/loved/no money worries/confidence due to material possessions
2 marks

d) i) Amit – good job
1 mark
Feel capable/intelligent/respected by others/intellectually challenged/all aid satisfactory self-concept
2 marks

ii) Sofiyah – intelligent/doing well at school
1 mark
Feel confident in her abilities/intellectually challenged/aid satisfactory self-concept development
2 marks

e) i) Amit – sexual orientation and family expectations
2 marks
Concern about parents finding out/worries for the future/feels less confident as a person because of his parents attitudes/not good enough to meet parents aspirations – self-esteem will be lowered
2 marks

ii) Sofiyah – gender expectations and family relationships
2 marks
Parents are less concerned about her future career because of her gender/parents seem to favour her brother
Self-concept lowered because of **both** factors
2 marks

f) Bullying at school
1 mark
Feel unwanted/disliked/trouble making friends – lose self-confidence/lower self-esteem and self-concept
2 marks

7. Expected
Expected
Unexpected
Expected
Unexpected
Expected
Unexpected
1 mark per answer = 7 marks

Total: 85 marks

1   Mr and Mrs Leung live with their children, Sarah, aged six months and Edward aged five. Mrs Leung's mother, who is 72, also lives with them.

a)   Name the **life stage** of

Mrs Leung's mother _____

_____

Edward _____

_____

Mr Leung _____

_____

Sarah _____

_____

(4 marks)

b)   The children demonstrate the following characteristics of **growth** and **development**.

Sarah can

- cry when she wants attention
- reach for a toy she wants
- sit up unsupported
- smile when she sees a member of the family

Match these characteristics to an area of development in the table

Physical characteristic	
Intellectual characteristic	
Emotional characteristic	
Social characteristic	

(4 marks)

c)   Edward can

- enjoy time spent with his grandparents when his parents are at work
- catch a ball
- play with his friend without arguing
- understand the rules of a board game

Match these characteristics to an area of development in the table

Physical characteristic	
Intellectual characteristic	
Emotional characteristic	
Social characteristic	

(4 marks)

d)   Name **two physical skills** Sarah will gain before she is one year old.

_____

_____

(2 marks)

e) Name **two intellectual skills** Sarah will gain before she is one year old.

_____

_____

(2 marks)

f) Mrs Leung's mother did not want to move in with the family, but was becoming too frail to live on her own.

Describe the effects on her **personal development** of moving in with the family.

_____

_____

_____

_____

_____

_____

_____

_____

_____

(4 marks)

2 Mr and Mrs Lever and their three teenage children are moving from London to live in the country. They are buying a house with some land around it. Mr Lever will work from home. The family will use the land to grow food for themselves. The house is in an isolated spot with no neighbours nearby. The children's school is a 30-minute bus ride away.

a) Identify **two social effects** on the children of the plan to move to the country. Describe how the effect you have identified will affect the children.

Effect 1. _____

_____

Description _____

_____

Effect 2. _____

_____

Description _____

_____

(4 marks)

b) The family are intending growing their own food. Describe the effects of this on:

i) their **physical health** _____

_____

_____

ii) their **economic circumstances** _____

_____

_____

(2 marks)

c) The family will now spend more time together because the house is isolated.

    i) Describe how this will have a **positive** effect on relationships between family members

_____

_____

_____

_____

_____

_____

_____

(4 marks)

    ii) Describe how this could have a **negative** effect on relationships between family members

_____

_____

_____

_____

_____

_____

_____

(4 marks)

d) The family will have less money than they used to have. Describe 4 ways that this could affect the **personal development** of the children.

1. _____

_____

_____

2. _____

_____

_____

3. _____

_____

_____

4. _____

_____

_____

(4 marks)

3 David is an only child. He is 17 years old. His parents divorced when he was baby. He has had little contact with his Dad as his Mum actively discouraged it. David regrets this. His mother is very protective of him. She has few friends and has made David the centre of her life. They live in a small village some miles from school so it was difficult for David to have a social life outside school. David is going to university in the autumn. He is looking forward to this. His Mum is not.

a) Identify two factors that have had a **negative** effect on David's personal development. Describe how each factor has affected him.

Factor 1. _____

_____

_____

Description _____

_____

_____

Factor 2. _____

_____

_____

Description _____

_____

_____

(4 marks)

b) Describe the **positive** effects that going to university will have on David's **personal development**.

_____

_____

_____

_____

(3 marks)

c) Describe the **negative** aspects of the relationship between David and his mother.

_____

_____

_____

_____

(3 marks)

d) Describe the effects on David's mother's **self-concept** when David leaves home.

_____

_____

_____

_____

(4 marks)

e) Identify David's life stage

_____

(1 mark)

f) Identify David's mother's life stage

_____

(1 mark)

4   Debbie is nineteen. She has recently moved into a flat with her friend. She has been promoted at the building society where she works. She was very pleased because she was the only woman among the six candidates for the job. Debbie felt more confident as she had recently started wearing contact lenses after years of wearing glasses, which she hated. Debbie has been going out with Mark for over a year. The relationship is very stable.

a) Identify Debbie's **life stage**.

_____

(1 mark)

b) Identify 5 factors that may affect the development of Debbie's **self-concept** at this life stage. Describe how each factor could affect her personal development.

Factor 1. _____

Possible effect. _____

_____

Factor 2. _____

Possible effect. _____

_____

Factor 3. _____

Possible effect. _____

_____

Factor 4. _____

Possible effect. _____

_____

Factor 5. _____

Possible effect. _____

_____

(10 marks)

c) Debbie has a **positive** relationship with Mark. Describe how this will affect her personal development.

_____

_____

_____

_____

_____

(3 marks)

5   Mr and Mrs Davis have been married for 48 years. Mr Davis is having problems with arthritis in his knees. Mrs Davis is in the first stages of Alzheimer's disease and she can no longer be left on her own. The couple have a home help called Margaret. Margaret used to come twice a week but now visits daily to make sure the couple are all right. Mr Davis knows that without Margaret, it is likely that either his wife or both of them would have to go into a residential home.

a) Describe 3 benefits to the Davis's of their relationship with Margaret.

Benefit 1. _____

_____

Benefit 2. _____

_____

Benefit 3. _____

_____

(3 marks)

b) Describe 2 **negative** effects of the relationship for Margaret.

Effect 1. _____

_____

Effect 2. _____

_____

(2 marks)

c) Describe how Mrs Davis's condition will affect the

   i) **Physical health** of Mr Davis _____

_____

_____

   ii) **Mental health** of Mr Davis. _____

_____

_____

(4 marks)

d) Identify 2 **professional carers or services** that could help support the Davis family at this time. Describe the form of support they offer.

Service 1. _____

_____

Description. _____

_____

Service 2. _____

_____

Description. _____

_____

(4 marks)

e) Describe 2 **voluntary** and **faith-based** services that could provide support to the Davis family. Describe the form of support they offer.

Service 1. _____

_____

Description. _____

_____

Service 2. _____

_____

Description. _____

_____

(4 marks)

f) The relationship between Mr and Mrs Davis may become **abusive**. Describe why this could happen.

_____

_____

_____

_____

_____

(3 marks)

g) Moving into a residential home is an example of an **unexpected life event**. Describe in terms of the PIES, what effect it could have on Mr Davis's **personal development**.

Physical development _____

_____

_____

Intellectual development _____

_____

_____

Emotional development _____

_____

_____

Social development _____

_____

_____

(4 marks)

Total: 92 marks

Practice marking scheme for OCR

1 **a)** Mrs Leung's mother – Later adulthood
   Edward – Child
   Mr Leung – Adult
   Sarah – Infant
   1 mark each = 4 marks

   b) Physical – Sit up unsupported
   Intellectual – Reach for a toy she wants
   Emotional – Cry when she wants attention
   Social – Smile when she sees a member of the family
   1 mark each = 4 marks

   c) Physical – Catch a ball
   Intellectual – Understand the rules of a board game
   Emotional – Enjoy time spent with his grandfather
   Social – Play with a friend without arguing
   1 mark each = 4 marks

   d) Crawling
   Walking holding onto someone
   Pull upright when holding onto something
   Drink from a cup
   (any)
   2 marks

   e) Understands 'no' and 'bye-bye' (any)
   Speaks 3 words
   Points out objects
   Responds to own name
   Looks for toy in the right direction
   (any)
   2 marks

   f) Increase contact with family members
   May lose feelings of independence
   May have more money
   May lose old friends from near previous home
   May have better diet because she no longer eats alone
   Has company of the family
   (any)
   4 marks

2 **a)** Effect – Lose contact with old friends in London
   1 mark
   Description – Feel lonely/miss friends
   1 mark
   Effect – Difficult to have a good social life in the new home due to isolated position
   1 mark
   Description – Feel isolated/more difficult to establish new friendships at the new school/lack social contact with peer group/may become closer to siblings.
   1 mark

   b) Physical health – Greater interest in diet/healthier
   More fruit and vegetables/healthier
   Any – 1 mark
   More exercise growing the crops/doing the gardening
   Economic circumstances – Save money by growing their own
   1 mark

c) Positive
- Family will become closer
- Family will get to know each other better
- Children will play/interact more
- Family will depend on each other more

(any)

4 marks

Negative
- Family will get tired of each other
- Family will need outside stimulation
- Family will become socially isolated
- Family may row more
- Each child will lack companions of their own peer group

(any)

4 marks

d) Children will not be able to buy as many possessions – may feel embarrassed/socially isolated

Children will not be able to go on trips or buy educational toys – may affect education

Children may not be able to join in the social life of the peer group – increase feelings of social isolation

Children may work harder because they have less distractions or because they want to make money for themselves – greater educational achievement

OR other relevant suggestion

Idea MUST include effect on a type of development (PIES)

4 marks

3 a) Two from – factors
- Divorced parents
- Little contact with father
- Little opportunities for social contact outside school
- Too close a relationship with mother

Two from – description
- Reduced chances for social contact
- No male role model
- Lone parent family may have had less money
- Little chance for development of independence
- Feeling of responsibility for mother's happiness
- Guilt at leaving mother to go to University

  1 mark for each factor identified plus **1 mark** for description of impact/effect on life opportunities/chances

  Total = 4 marks

b) Possible benefits include
- Independence from mother
- Better social life
- Educational opportunity
- Chance to improve relationship with Dad

(any)

3 marks

c) Negative aspects
- Relationship too close/stifling
- David feels guilt at mother's dependence on him to make her happy
- Lack of balance with a father figure
- The family is socially isolated by geography/mother's lack of friendships

(any)

3 marks

d) Possible effects on self-concept
- Loss of role
- Able to build her own life
- Feels powerless to prevent David moving away
- Loss of sense of purpose
- Frightened for future without him

4 marks – high level answer should include 2 possible effects on mother's self-concept, accurately explained. Explanation accompanied by clear reasoning.

1–2 marks – low-level answer has only 1 effect without clear understanding of self-concept.

e) Life stage – adolescence
1 mark

f) Life stage – adulthood
1 mark

4 **a)** Life stage – adulthood
1 mark

b) Five from
- Age
- Appearance
- Gender
- Emotional development
- Education
- Relationships with others
- Life experiences

5 marks

Plus **1 mark** for each appropriate description of impact/effect on personal development
Total = 10 marks

c) Sense of emotional stability
Someone to confide in/share problems
Improvement of social life
Satisfactory sexual relationship
(any)
3 marks

5 **a)** Receive emotional support
Provides companionship
Provides practical help e.g. shopping
Provides advice and guidance
Provides social contact
(any)
3 marks

b) May resent increasing dependence on her
Physically tiring
Less time for own family/friends
May be frightened of the responsibility
(any)
2 marks

c) **i)** Physical health
- He has to do more for her which will tire him out
- Cannot leave her, so she has to escort him everywhere/physically tiring
- He has to do more in the house which will aggravate his arthritis
Any – 2 marks

ii) Mental health
- Stress of caring for her
- Concern for the future
- Sadness at the 'loss' of personality – depressing
- Constant worry of what she might do to harm herself or their home
- Lack of conversation due to her condition – lack of intellectual stimulation
  Any – 2 marks

d) Two from
- Social Services – Assessment
- Community nursing – Direct care
- GP services – Physical and mental health check
- Mental health services – Monitoring
1 mark for each service and **1 mark** for description of their support. **Total = 4 marks**

e) Two from
- Age Concern – Emotional support/financial advice
- Help the Aged – Emotional support/financial advice
- Local charity concerned with care of the elderly – support/practical help
- Vicar/priest/local religious leader – counselling/support/befriending service
- Meals on Wheels – help with daily meal
  OR other relevant suggestions
1 mark for service and **1 mark** for description of support offered. **Total = 4 marks**

f) Reasons include
- Loss of patience with her condition
- Tired/exhaustion due to increased care needed by her
- Frustration with the condition
- He is physically stronger than her – could force her to do things
- Tired/exhaustion due to his own medical condition
  Any – 3 marks

g) Physical development – may eat and sleep better due to care provided
Intellectual development – May have increased stimulation due to company of others
or may lack stimulation now he no longer has to look after the family and the home.
Emotional development – may miss companionship of his wife
Social development – may form new friendships among other residents **or** may miss
old friends and neighbours
1 mark per suggestion = **4 marks**

Total: 92 marks

Practice exam paper for AQA

1 The Hayes family consists of Mark aged 39, Emily aged 38 and their children Jon aged 14, Susie aged 9 and Beth aged 1. Mr Hayes's father, Wilfred, aged 72, also lives with the family.

    a) Identify the **life stages** of each family member. The first is done for you.

- Beth (1) Infancy _____
- Jon (14) _____
- Wilfred (72) _____
- Emily (38) _____
- Mark (39) _____
- Susie (9) _____

(5 marks)

    b) Describe **2 intellectual** changes that will happen to Beth over the next three years.

1. _____

_____

2. _____

_____

(2 marks)

    c) Describe **3 physical** changes that will happen to Susie in the next seven years.

1. _____

_____

2. _____

_____

3. _____

_____

(3 marks)

    d) Beth has formed an **attachment relationship** with her parents. Explain what is meant by an attachment relationship.

_____

_____

_____

_____

(2 marks)

2 Nadia is 45. She is married to Bill

- She has just started to experience the first stages of the menopause.
- Nadia's parents died several years ago.
- Bill has just taken early retirement from work
- Nadia's younger sister recently died in a car crash.
- Nadia and Bill are moving house to be near their niece and nephew, now their mother has died.

a) Identify **3** expected life events from the information given.

1. _____

2. _____

3. _____

(3 marks)

b) Identify **2** unexpected life events from the information given.

1. _____

2. _____

(2 marks)

c) Explain the possible effects of retirement on Bill's **social** and **intellectual** health and well-being.

_____

_____

_____

_____

_____

(3 marks)

d) Nadia was very upset at her sister's death. At such a time, sources of support can help people cope with life events.

Identify **two professional** carers and support services that could help Nadia at this time. Suggest how each type of support may help Nadia.

Source 1. _____

_____

May help by _____

_____

Source 2. _____

_____

May help by _____

_____

(4 marks)

e) Identify **two voluntary or faith-based** services that could help Nadia at this time. Suggest how each type of support may help her.

Source 1. _____

_____

May help by _____

_____

Source 2. _____

_____

May help by _____

_____

(4 marks)

3 Maggie and Steve live together. They are getting married next year.

- Steve is a foreman at a garage.
- Michael is one of the mechanics at the garage
- Damien is Michael's father
- Michael is planning a holiday in Ibiza with Paul.

a) Identify and describe the different relationships described above

Maggie and Steve _____

_____

_____

_____

_____

(2 marks)

Steve and Michael _____

_____

_____

_____

_____

(2 marks)

Damien and Michael _____

_____

_____

_____

_____

(2 marks)

Michael and Paul _____

_____

_____

_____

_____

(2 marks)

b) Michael and Paul have a **positive** relationship. Describe how this will affect Michael's:

i) Emotional development. _____

_____

_____

_____

(2 marks)

ii) Social development. _____

_____

_____

_____

(2 marks)

c) Michael and Steve do not get on. They have a **negative** relationship. Describe how this will affect Michael's **personal** development.

_____

_____

_____

_____

_____

(4 marks)

4 Jordan is Chinese. His **culture** is one factor that affects his self-concept.

List six other factors that may affect Jordan's self-concept. For each factor, explain how it may affect him positively.

Factor 1 _____

How it would affect him positively.

_____

_____

(2 marks)

Factor 2 _____

How it would affect him positively.

_____

_____

(2 marks)

Factor 3 _____

How it would affect him positively.

_____

_____

(2 marks)

Factor 4 _____

How it would affect him positively.

_____

_____

(2 marks)

Factor 5 _____

How it would affect him positively.

_____

_____

(2 marks)

Factor 6 _____

How it would affect him positively.

_____

_____

(2 marks)

5 Mandy is seventeen. She lives with her parents and younger brother. She lives in a large house with a garden. Her parents are in full-time, professional jobs. Mandy has serious asthma.

   a) What is Mandy's life stage? _____

   (1 mark)

   b) What is **self-esteem**? _____

   _____

   (1 mark)

   c) Explain how the following factors will affect Mandy's **self-esteem.**

   Her home. _____

   _____

   _____

   (2 marks)

   Her asthma. _____

   _____

   _____

   (2 marks)

   Her relationship with other family members. _____

   _____

   _____

   (2 marks)

   d) What is meant by **employment prospects**? _____

   _____

   (2 marks)

   e) Explain how the following factors will affect her employment prospects.

   Her parents' jobs. _____

   _____

   (2 marks)

   Her education. _____

   _____

   (2 marks)

   Her asthma. _____

   _____

   (2 marks)

6 Sheila is a single parent and lives with Terry.

   • The family lives on benefits
   • Shelia has two children, Darren aged 13 and Sean aged 7
   • Sean has started refusing to go to school

   a) **Identify** and **describe** Shelia's and Terry's relationship

   _____

   _____

   _____

   (2 marks)

b) Give reasons why Sean could become a victim of **child abuse**.

_____

_____

_____

(3 marks)

c) Describe the effects **abuse** and **neglect** can have on the **personal development** of a young child.

_____

_____

_____

_____

(5 marks)

Total: 82 marks

1 **a)** Jon – Adolescent
         Wilfred – Later adulthood
         Emily – Adulthood
         Mark – Adulthood
         Susie –Childhood
         5 marks

   b) Any **two** of the following
         Learn to talk
         Recognise numbers
         Recognise letters
         Can write own name
         Can colour in shaded areas of pictures
         2 marks

   c) Any **three** of the following
         Breasts grow
         Periods start
         Hips widen
         Pubic hair grows
         3 marks

   d) A **secure emotional** relationship between the child and main carers
         Necessary for satisfactory emotional and social development
         2 marks

2 **a)** Nadia is married
         Nadia is experiencing the menopause
         Nadia's parents have died
         Bill has just retired
         Any – 3 marks

   b) Nadia's sister has died
         Nadia and Bill are moving house
         2 marks

   c) Loss of friendships from work
         Loss of stimulation from work
         Loss of social activities from work
         Reduced income may mean fewer opportunities for social events
         May have opportunity to take up new interests/hobbies
         Any – 3 marks

   d) GP – Medication
         Counsellor – Bereavement counselling
         Social worker – Help with bereavement
         Source – **2 marks**
         Help (correctly matched to source of help) – **2 marks**

   e) Local religious leader e.g. vicar, priest – counselling/befriending service
         National charity e.g. Cruise – counselling/practical help/befriending service
         Local self-help group for the bereaved – counselling/practical help/befriending service
         Source – **2 marks**
         Help (correctly matched to source of help) – **2 marks**

3   a   Maggie and Steve
        Identifies intimate/sexual relationship
        Reference to sexual nature of relationship
        2 marks
        Steve and Michael
        Identification of working relationship
        As boss and worker
        2 marks
        Damien and Michael
        Identification of family relationship
        As father and son
        2 marks
        Michael and Paul
        Identification of friendship relationship
        As friends going away together/spending free time together
        2 marks

    b) Emotional development
        Someone to talk to
        Someone to confide in
        Someone to discuss problems with
        Someone to share success with
        Any – 2 marks
        Social development
        Someone to go out with
        Someone to go away with
        Someone to share new experiences with
        Any – 2 marks

    c) Personal development
        Michael will not enjoy work – Intellectual
        Michael will not work hard – Intellectual
        Michael will not feel able to confide any problems in his boss – Emotional
        Michael may not go to work/phone in sick when not ill – Intellectual
        Michael may feel resentment at others successes because he feels they are due to
        favouritism – emotional
        Michael will not perform well at work – emotional
        Any – 4 marks

4   Identification of the six factors, followed by explanations of the contributions of each
    factor which will be positive statements relating to increased self-concept/self-
    confidence/self-esteem.
    Appearance/how he looks: increased confidence if he looks good, then feels good.
    Gender: confidence in gender role leading to increased self-confidence etc.
    Emotional development/developmental maturity: confidence-increasing self-
    assertiveness
    Education/schooling: gain confidence from understanding/knowledge/developing skills.
    Relationships with others: confidence from social acceptance/support of others raises
    self-esteem
    Sexual orientation: comfortable with gender role/confidence in relationships
    Life experiences: confidence gained from learning/development/wisdom of experience
    raises self-confidence
    Any – 6 marks for identification of factor
    6 marks for correct match with explanation
    Total = 12 marks

5 **a)** Mandy's life stage – adolescent
  1 mark

 b) Self-esteem – How good you feel about yourself
  1 mark

 c) Her home – Will feel good because she can invite people home/feel pride in her home
  2 marks
  Her asthma – May feel embarrassment due to the condition/feel worth less than others due to her illness/may prevent her from taking part in activities so increasing feelings of isolation
  Any – 2 marks
  Relationships with family members – would increase self-esteem as she has good relationships with people important to her/help self-confidence as she has people to confide in/share problems with
  Any – 2 marks

 d) Employment prospects – your chances of getting and keeping a satisfying, well paid, stimulating job.
  2 marks

 e) Parent's jobs – provide example of what can be achieved/she may strive to achieve the same/she may want the financial rewards that she now enjoys for herself as an adult so that she works hard
  Any – 2 marks
  Her education – Success at school should lead to qualifications to enable her to get a good job/lack of success would lead to poor qualifications so that employment prospects would not be as good
  2 marks
  Her asthma – May lead to time off work due to illness/medical appointments
  May lead to lack of confidence due to the condition which holds her back/limits her ambitions
  2 marks

6 **a)** Shelia and Terry
  Identification of intimate personal relationship
  Reference to sexual nature of the relationship
  2 marks

 b) Reasons for possible abuse
  Step-parent relationship
  Lack of money
  Frustration at Sean's school refusal
  Stress of financial situation taken out on child
  3 marks

 c) Physical – poor diet/lack of warmth   Social effects
  Hygiene problems   Lack of social interaction difficulties in
  Increased chances of illness   forming relationships
  Poor physical growth/failure too thrive   Difficulties with normal social behaviour
  Emotional effects   patterns
  Insecurity   Intellectual effects
  Emotional withdrawal   Learning difficulties
                                                  Examples of difficulties e.g. reading/numeracy

  Answers should include an example from each type of development
  5 marks

Total: 82 marks

WORK PLACEMENT DIARY

Name: _____

School: _____

School telephone number: _____

Work placement details

Address:

_____

_____

_____ **Tel:** _____

Name of supervisor: _____

Describe the work place:

_____

_____

_____

_____

_____

_____

Take a photograph of both the inside and the outside of the building to include in your portfolio if you have access to a camera.

Draw a labelled ground plan of the working environment:

Interview your supervisor

1. What service/s do you provide?

   _____
   _____
   _____
   _____

2. Which client group/s do you serve?

   _____

3. What are the needs of your clients?

   a. Physical: _____
   b. Intellectual: _____
   c. Emotional: _____
   d. Social: _____

4. Which care sector do you belong in? (statutory, voluntary, private or not-for-profit)

   _____
   _____
   _____

5. How is the service funded?

   _____
   _____
   _____
   _____

6. How does funding at national levels affect your service?

   _____
   _____
   _____
   _____

7. How does funding at local level affect your service? Do you have targets to meet?

   _____
   _____
   _____
   _____

8. How is the service organised so that clients can use it?

   _____
   _____
   _____

9. How is the service delivered so that clients can use it?

_____

_____

_____

_____

10. Why is this service provided?

_____

_____

_____

_____

11. Why is it based here?

_____

_____

_____

_____

12. Which codes of practice do you use?

_____

_____

_____

_____

13. Which charters do you use?

_____

_____

_____

_____

14. What policies do you have?

_____

_____

_____

_____

15. Can I have a copy of some of your codes of practice, policies and charters please?

16. Can I have a copy of any leaflets or adverts about this service please?
(Make sure you keep them safe to put in your portfolio.)

17. Am I allowed to take photographs of the client?

_____

Direct care workers

Pick two direct care workers you are working with (they should have different job titles). Find out the following information about each of them.

Person 1

Name: _____

Job title: _____

Qualifications: _____

Route to getting the qualifications:

_____

Disadvantages and/or advantages of this route:

_____

_____

Alternative ways to get the qualifications:

_____

_____

Qualities needed to do the job:

_____

_____

_____

_____

Skills needed to do the job:

_____

_____

_____

_____

Tasks done on a typical day:

_____

_____

_____

_____

_____

_____

_____

_____

_____

_____

_____

Direct care workers

Pick two direct care workers you are working with (they should have different job titles).
Find out the following information about each of them.

Person 2

Name: _____

Job title: _____

Qualifications: _____

Route to getting the qualifications:

_____

Disadvantages and/or advantages of this route:

_____

_____

Alternative ways to get the qualifications:

_____

_____

Qualities needed to do the job:

_____

_____

_____

Skills needed to do the job:

_____

_____

_____

Tasks done on a typical day:

_____

_____

_____

_____

_____

_____

_____

_____

_____

_____

Your work

Write details of what **you** do – add more pieces of paper if you need to:

_____

_____

_____

_____

_____

_____

_____

_____

_____

_____

_____

_____

_____

_____

_____

_____

_____

_____

_____

_____

_____

_____

_____

_____

_____

_____

_____

_____

_____

_____

_____

_____

_____

_____

_____

Communication skills

Make notes of conversations you have with clients that demonstrate you have used **relevant communication skills** (non verbal communication – body language, listening skills – or verbal communication – asking questions). Talk to clients about the service provided and ask how they feel about the service provided.

_____
_____
_____
_____
_____
_____
_____
_____
_____
_____
_____
_____
_____
_____
_____
_____
_____

If you are allowed to take your camera in, have your photo taken with various people (clients and care workers) that show you using your communication skills.

Ask the care workers which **barriers to communication** they have met e.g. visual or hearing disability, environmental (lighting, noise, size of group etc.), language difficulties, physical disabilities, learning or memory disability, misunderstanding etc. and how they try to overcome these.

_____
_____
_____
_____
_____
_____
_____
_____
_____
_____
_____
_____

Interview a care worker about the care value base

1. How is anti-discrimatory practice used to support your clients? Can you give some examples?

   _____

   _____

   _____

   _____

   _____

   _____

   _____

   _____

   _____

2. While working with clients how do you ensure **equality** of care and at the same time recognise that we are all different people with different needs and backgrounds? (This is the **diversity** of the care value base.) Please give some examples.

   _____

   _____

   _____

   _____

   _____

   _____

   _____

   _____

   _____

3. What kinds of **confidential** issues might arise in your workplace? How do you maintain confidentiality?

   _____

   _____

   _____

   _____

   _____

   _____

   _____

   _____

   _____

   _____

4. How are clients protected from abuse?

_____
_____
_____
_____
_____
_____

5. How do you build relationships with the clients? Can you give some examples?

_____
_____
_____
_____
_____
_____

6. How do you make sure you communicate fully with clients? Can you give some examples?

_____
_____
_____
_____
_____
_____

7. How do you provide individual care for each client?

_____
_____
_____
_____
_____
_____

8. How do you promote and support the rights of each individual? Can you give examples?

_____
_____
_____
_____
_____
_____

Appendix 2: Key Skills mapping grid

Many of the worksheets in this file give students the opportunity to provide either some evidence that they have used one or more of the Key Skills successfully, or give them practice in this. The grid below identifies those opportunities. It does not include worksheets that are felt not to have any such use or the assignment sheets. There are plenty of opportunities to use Key Skills in the portfolio assignments but the level of these will vary according to how each student tackles them.

Title of worksheet	Core work	Extension activity
Portfolio skills		
Putting together a portfolio		
Code of conduct	C1.1, 2.1, IT1.2	
Collecting evidence	C1.1, 2.1	C1.2, 1.3, 2.3, 2.4
Conducting a survey	C1.1, 2.1, WO1.1, 1.2, 1.3, IT1.2	IT2.3
Get it taped	C1.1, 2.1, WO1.1, 1.2, 1.3	
In your own words	C1.2, 1.3	C2.3
Talk it over	C2.1	
Find it out	C1.1, 2.3, IT1.1, 2.1	
A plan of action	C1.1, 2.1, WO1.1, 1.2, 2.1, 2.2, PS1.1	
A balanced diet	C1.2, 1.3, 2.3, 2.4, IT1.2, 2.3	
Unit 1		
Services for adolescents	IT1.2, 2.1	WO2.1, 2.2, C2.2
Services for adults	C1.2	C2.3, 1.3
Policy making	C1.1, 2.1	
Social policy goals		
Health needs assessment		
Local statutory services	C1.2	C2.1, IT1.2, 2.3
Voluntary organisations	IT1.1, 1.2, 2.1, 2.2, WO1.1, 1.2, 1.3, 2.1, 2.3, C1.1, 1.2, 2.1	
Funding services	C1.1, 2.1	
Barriers to use of services	C1.2, 1.3	
Barriers to communication		IT1.1, 2.1
Different communication needs of children	C1.2	C1.1, 2.1, WO 1.1, 1.2, 1.3, 2.1, 2.2, 2.3
Different communication needs of disabled people	C1.3	C2.4
The balance between action and inaction	C1.1, 2.1	WO1.2, 2.2
Promoting anti-discriminatory practice	LP2.2	
The effects of discrimination	C1.1, 2.1	C2.3

Title of worksheet	Core work	Extension activity
Written communication	C1.1	C2.4
Maintaining confidentiality	C1.1	C2.1, WO2.1
Unit 2		
PIES for adolescents	C1.1, 1.2, 1.3	
PIES for older people		C1.3
PIES for disabled people	C1.2	
Knowledge check on PIES	C1.2	
Risk management in school	WO1.1, 1.2	IT1.1, 1.2, 2.1, C2.2
Risk management in health and social care settings	C1.1, 2.1, WO1.1, 1.2	C2.2, IT2.3, WO2.2, 2.3
Genetically inherited diseases and conditions: cystic fibrosis	IT1.1	
Solvent abuse	C1.2	C1.1, 2.1
Smoking	C1.1, 2.1, IT1.2, 2.2, 2.3	WO1.1, 1.2, 1.3, LP1.1, 1.2
HIV/AIDS	N1.1, 1.2, 1.3	N2.2
Height and weight charts	N1.1, C1.3	
Blood pressure	C1.1	C2.1
Body Mass Index	C1.1	IT1.2, C2.1
Resting pulse rate and recovery after exercise	N1.1	
Health promotion	C1.2, 1.3	IT2.2
Unit 3		
Using a centile chart	N1.1	
Earnings of men and women	N1.1, 1.2, 1.3	
Living in a lone-parent family	C1.1, C2.1a	
Marriages and divorces	N1.2, 1.3	